CHAPTER I

I wrote three thousand words last night, but I inadvertently deleted them today before I came next door to the grocery to have a chicken salad sandwich and get their WiFi password. But it's probably a good thing, because last night I was writing while I was extremely intoxicated on a THC-infused gummy candy. Most would've probably thought I was making "word salad" (although the severity of such a claim could be debated). And this rabbi I really like listening to claims that marijuana isn't kosher. He says you can perform a mitzvah while drunk because alcohol only changes your mood (and makes you care less) while marijuana alters your mind, so if you do perform a mitzvah while high, it doesn't count or something. Of course, there is no one "Jewish" opinion on almost anything. So, who knows? I can jive with what he says, though. Marijuana gives me tremendous anxiety and a flood of negative thoughts sometimes. Still, three thousand words. That was a lot. I was pretty proud of myself.

The two lovely proprietors of this store are talking about a newspaper article one of them read about two people being involved in a crash. I don't really know anyone here except for my friend that I'm staying with. She asks that her alias be Adelaide. I'm not too into this chicken salad sandwich, although I can see how many would find it delicious. It just has too many crunchy things for my taste, I think.

So yeah, I first met Adelaide when I was in fourth grade. We were sitting on the ground in the car rider line, and I asked her what her name was. I was surprised she spoke in such a "Yankee" accent, so that always stood out in my memory. There was just something about her, too. Even though we didn't really become good acquaintances or friends until high school, I think I knew that we would reconnect again. She doesn't remember this, though. Of course, she was a couple years younger than me, which is a lot when you're in elementary school.

This whole deal about changing names or knowing what to write or not write is going to be really frustrating. Maybe I should just write what's in my head and let an editor deal with the rest.

A man just came in asking if they sold cigarettes. They don't. I feel bad for the owners. This is kind of a touristy stop in a very neglected area, and their business has been pretty bad since Covid started. Nice people, though. They have all kinds of interesting things–the perfect place to buy someone a gift. Oh, that's right. It's Purim. I'm supposed to buy two food gifts for one friend and give something to two poor people. Maybe if I buy food for two poor people it will count. How do you define poor, though? Does this mitzvah even count since I'm not Jewish? I don't think it would hurt anything. If I were rich I'd celebrate Purim every day.

I really don't want to finish the last fourth of my sandwich, but I don't want to be rude. I told the lady she should make some pimento cheese, and she said she tried over the Winter, but it wasn't a big success. I would definitely buy it, though. I'm surprised anyone would even have it this far north. I'm not sure what Southern Indiana would be considered geo-culturally or whatever. It's kind of mid-Western and kind of Southern. I don't mind it. Although I'd like to go hang out in Louisville sometime. The gummies came from Michigan, by the way. It's legal there now. I think I can finish it–slowly but surely. I wouldn't mind some candy, though. They have an excellent selection of old-fashioned candies. I would send some Mary Janes to my dad, but the last time I checked for them on the Internet I found there must be some kind of production issue. Oh well.

I just realized how many gun-related items they have here. They do like their guns in Southern Indiana, I've heard. To each his own—as long as they're not used to shoot me or anyone I love—or anyone at all, really. Such a touchy subject. I've had several best friends die due to guns, so yeah.

Cheri was the first. I was living out in the middle of nowhere at this old plantation house we called "The Farm". This awesome and rich Jewish teenager was supporting me and several other people with her daddy's credit card. I was in my mid-20s, and Cheri was about 40. Cheri's daughter had left a copy of her Left 4 Dead video game at The Farm, and they had gone over there to get it back, but someone had hidden it. Cheri called me and asked me what to do (I was in Atlanta at the time).

I told her not to take any shit. I can't remember my exact words. But apparently shortly after I got off the phone with her, her son had a gun in his hand, and it went off and shot her between the eyes. I drove over 100 mph all the way to the hospital in Macon, livid. I was going to kill Allen—well, not literally, but I was clearly extremely upset. I found him, and he was just a mess. He asked me if I had a Xanax, which I didn't. They took me back to see Cheri . Her head was all bandaged up. Then her leg twitches. I got really excited, but they told me that it was involuntary muscle movements. She was gone. I can't remember why they were keeping her alive.

The ride to her funeral was pretty rough. I think we listened to "The Funeral" by Bands of Horses. That song now reminds me of my uncle's funeral, too—his name was Johnny.

Anyway, after the funeral we had this big party at The Farm. Allen came. I hugged him in one of the bedrooms for a while. The GBI ended up investigating me because they thought I had something to do with it all. The only thing I could figure out is that maybe they suspected Allen and I had something going on. But if that were the case, Cheri would've been thrilled. So that's bullshit.

I ended up writing a short story about it for Creative Loafing. I didn't win. I thought it was a little trashy, although Steven said it was sultry or smoky or something–can't remember the exact adjective he used. Steven was one of our housemates at The Farm.

I kind of have to poop, so I think I'm going to go now. I also only have half of a cigarette left. I've been meaning to quit, but it just hasn't happened yet. Maybe I should try again today. I would take the Mercedes to town to buy a pack, but it smells like gas and makes me nauseous.

Okay, I pooped. I feel better. Now I'm back in my bed, and I'm out of cigarettes, even though there are at least six empty packs beside me. It's also a little chilly up here, but the heater makes a weird noise when I turn it on, so I'm kind of scared to use it. I'm going downstairs.

Alright, I'm in the living room now in a recliner that won't recline because it's too close to the wall. We picked it up the day I bought the gummies. I really need to find somewhere comfortable to write. Maybe I shouldn't have left the store. Pooping is dumb but also awesome. There is a cat sniffing my shoe. Should I eat another gummy? I know my mother would be completely against the idea. But it does help with my creativity.

My mind is just a lot quieter when I'm sober, since I'm on a pretty heavy-duty anti-psychotic. It's Purim, though. Some people get as drunk as possible so that they don't know the difference between good Mordechai and bad Haman. I don't really know the difference between them sober, though. I mean, I kind of do, but not much. Now there is a large dog sniffing me. The other medium-sized dog keeps pawing at me. I think they want to play or something.

I really want a cigarette. I have $7.06 left on my card. Should I do it? I'm just not really ready to quit. I don't want to quit, even though I've gotten several potential signs from the Universe or God or something that I should. I really can't deal with that gasoline smell, though. Oh awesome, Adelaide said I can take the truck instead.

Ok, I got a pack. I feel better, even though I really wish I could work up the will to quit smoking for good. My therapist in Bethlehem (Pennsylvania–I used to live in Allentown) referred me to a rabbi at the oldest gay synagogue in NYC, who told me I should keep the mitzvot and learn Hebrew. Or maybe my therapist said that. I don't remember. The rabbi did tell me that the cut-off line for the prohibition of homosexuality is anal sex, though–not that I have anyone in mind for that. Maybe I should eat a gummy. Baby steps.

I just called my mom and told her I needed money for Purim. She controls my finances now that I'm on Disability. I'm okay with that usually. I'm terrible with money. I only make a little over $1000 per month, so I have to be careful. At least I don't have a bad addiction to anything expensive anymore– other than cigarettes. At least it's not opiates. Opiate addictions are ridiculously expensive. I really, really want to eat a gummy, but according to the rabbi, my mitzvot wouldn't count if I did. How sad. I wonder if he's right. Are cigarettes a mind-altering substance–well, at least the nicotine? They should have a nicotine rehab. I've been smoking an average of a pack a day since about 1999. That's a long time. Is Jagermeister kosher? I heard once that it had deer's blood in it, but somehow I doubt that's true. Maybe it did at one point. I could Google it, I guess. But I was going to try to restrain myself from Googling while I write this book.

The bottle has a cross on it. That's interesting. I could write several chapters on theology. Maybe I should start now. Maybe not. I should probably have some sort of outline, but I don't. I already mentioned my other friends who got shot, so I feel like if anything I should write about them first. I mean, they're definitely not my only friends who have died. I have had many. This is why I feel like I need drugs. It's stressful to think about some of these things, you know?

I broke down and Googled Jager. It's kosher, supposedly. Maybe I should have a shot or two. And a cigarette.

Ok, I talked to my mom. She put $50 on my card. I asked Adelaide, and she said she and her dad are considered poor, so I'm waiting for her response to know what kind of food I should buy. I have to do it before sundown. Maybe today is the day I start trying to keep all the mitzvot. I remember hearing something about a correlation between that and Purim, I think. That means that I won't be able to write after sundown, since it'll be the Sabbath, and you're not supposed to do any work or light a fire, both of which could be said of what I am doing (the work part is debatable, but a spark is a type of fire, right?). Orthodox Jews would agree. Whether or not they would agree to my attempts of completing mitzvot, I'm not so sure.

Meanwhile, I'm going to listen to the Megillat Esther in Hebrew for the second time. That's one of the three mitzvot for Purim, according to the rabbi I've been watching. I wish I could understand what they were singing. It's really, really long. Maybe I should just be a goy. I want a cigarette.

I should probably Google what kind of work is actually prohibited on the Sabbath–or what is considered "work", that is. Apparently you can't play an instrument, which is kind of sad. What am I supposed to do? It would be different if I had a Jewish family or something–there would probably be plenty of things to do.

There is this passage in Isaiah that I really identify with. It mentions eunuchs and how they will be blessed if they keep the Sabbaths. There is a Kaballistic interpretation that states that if one studies the Torah during the week and has sex with his wife on the Sabbath, he will have holy children. While I would love to have a family, I'm not entirely sure that my body would ever allow me to make babies with someone with a vagina.

Adelaide wants to go to dinner later with her friend Timmy, but that'll probably be after sundown. What to do, what to do?

Actually, she just got home. That's cool.

Well we went to Walmart, and I bought some Japanese food for Adelaide and me and White Castle for her dad. She got a Crazy Girl Roll and I got hibachi. The hibachi was okay. The roll would've been delicious, but it has eel in it, so I didn't partake. I really need to get this religion thing sorted out.

So I think I might eat a piece of candy. I'm thinking about doing one sober chapter and one high chapter per day. Plus I've been told that you shouldn't actually keep the Sabbath unless you're Jewish. I don't know whether or not I'll regret this decision later. I'm almost done listening to Megillat. At least I've done three mitzvot today. That's something. Actually I'm a little nervous about eating another gummy. I don't know if people will hate me for whatever comes out of my mind. We'll see what happens, I guess.

The dogs are playing tug-of-war with an old rope toy. That's what my mind feels like. Adelaide said to do whatever feels right. I don't know if I should eat one. My mom would definitely be against the idea, although I'm not sure what God would think, if God has an opinion on the matter. Or really, I'm not completely certain that there is a god, although sometimes I think there is. Existence is really hard. I just had a suicidal thought. Did I mention I've been hospitalized for psychiatric reasons nine times? Fuck it, I guess.

Okay, my gummies were downstairs, so I ate a piece of Waterberry hard candy. I'm going to jump in the shower and loosen up. Maybe once it kicks in I'll be writing again.

CHAPTER II

I took a shower. I don't know how long it's been, but the candy hasn't kicked in yet. I was going to watch some porn because I feel like I need a release of endorphins, but I have guilt feelings about doing that. I'm listening to Alternative 90s music on YouTube Music. Maybe I should write about the 90s, even though that triggered a thought about the time I lived with porn stars in Huntington Beach. That was the summer of 2000, though. Don't leave me high. Don't leave me dry. Don't leave me high. Don't leave me dry. Le sigh.

The 90s. Well, I was born on Hitler's birthday in 1982, so I don't have too many memories of the 80s other than my grandparents and Snuggles bear and Hilton Head with Traci Nobles, who became a bit of a public figure briefly after a scandal with Anthony Weiner. I had his nude picture a year before anyone else. She called me before she went on Good Morning America or one of those shows. She was so nervous. I was very proud of her, though. That whole incident was pretty shady. I know if I write about what I know, many more people will want to read this. But I wouldn't want Traci to get upset (not that she did anything wrong at all). I still would like to know what Karl Lagerfeld had to do with all of that. Like, why would he befriend her? I understand why Hugh Hefner wanted her in Playboy. She's hot. But yeah. Not my business, really. I miss Traci. She is married now–or getting married. And she's sober. Good for her. Our moms have been best friends since they were teenagers. We used to vacation at their boss's beach house that used to be owned by Cher and Sonny Alman. Well, I think Capitol Records owned it, but they stayed there.

I don't really feel high, but you never know. I mean, I can feel maybe a slight difference. I don't think it's been long enough for anything more. Nine Inch Nails is going off. They remind me of the many hours a day I spent chatting on IRC back in the 90s. Oh yeah, the 90s.

I had one friend in the early 90s. **REDACTED**. I was in Boy Scouts, but I dropped out because I questioned why you had to say "thank you" after you give someone a knife rather than before. I don't know why that was such a pressing concern for me. But it was. I never really felt like I fit in at Boy Scouts, though. Probably because I was the only queer. **REDACTED** actually stopped having anything to do with me when people started saying that about me.

Once we were camping in the mountains, and the adults were gone. **REDACTED** told me to take off my clothes and run around the cabin, so I did. Later that night, I peeked through his boxers because I wanted to know if he had pubes. I didn't think it was fair that he got to see me. I'm not really sure if he knows that or how he would feel about it if he did, but we talked about Jesus for a long time the other night.

Better Man by Pearl Jam is on. This reminds me of my good friend Art. Art is this really awesome physically disabled punk. He has excellent taste in music. He is in a wheelchair. His dog died not too long ago, but he got a new pup. I am happy for him. I hung out with him and Jessica Legg a few weeks ago or something and drank. Jessica has this really old house behind her trailer. I want to go metal detecting there, but there's so much trash.

Oh yeah, the 90s. Comedown by Bush is playing. I'm reminded of Ottawa. July 1, 1997. That was an amazing day. Holly McNarland played at Parliament Hill or whatever. We ate at Nickel's diner. I think Celine Dion owned it or something. It was the first time I ever rode a bus. I miss riding buses and subways and public transportation in general. I've lived all over the country, by the way.

There was this girl named Alix that I had a huge crush on, but no one knew. I had met all of these people on IRC, by the way. My dad had done something fucked up, I think, so he paid for my love by taking me on a trip up the coast. I held my first hand and lost my virginity on the same day to a boy named Brandon in Wachapreague, Virginia. That tunnel was crazy long. Oh yeah, he ended up being a porn star (huge peen), which is how I ended up in Huntington Beach, basically.

I hooked up with this famous gay porn star Ashton Ryan (that's his stage name), even though he had a boyfriend. We lived at 8th and Olive, I think. Kira lived in HB, too. Sadness was her name on IRC. We hung out a couple times. She's a really cool girl. I wonder what she would think about me using real names in my book.

The Cure is playing. First thought was this underground bar I went to in West Hollywood. oh, it also reminds me of this basement club in Manhattan, I think, where you could smoke cigarettes while listening to music like this and Belle & Sebastian. Did you know it's like this big Cholo thing in Los Angeles to listen to Morissey but not The Smiths? Weird. I learned that from frequenting The Eagle, which is an awesome leather/bear bar with pool tables. I've had some wild times there, for sure.

Brick by Ben Folds Five. He has my name. Although I was going to use a pseudonym. Hmm. Jupiter Davidson is what I was thinking. People that know me know that I have good reasons, so they say it's not pretentious. She's a brick and I'm drowning slowly, off the coast and I'm headed nowhere.

I'd love to be off the coast, although I don't want to drown. I pace a lot, too. Ashley (Alli on IRC) bought me roses in 1997. I think that may have been the only flowers anyone has ever given me. I was so in love with her. Now she's married with kids and has a good job and stuff. I freaked out once when I was off my meds and demanded for her to stop everything she was doing, buy a plane ticket, and meet me in Atlanta. But she didn't. So I blocked her, even though she told me if I blocked her she'd still be thinking of me.

I'm so fucked up. Now there's a flood of memories attached to that memory.

What's next? Rage Against the Machine. I saw them live at Mcarthur Park in LA. I think one of my roommates had something to do with a festival they were having there or something. I can't remember. I was never a huge fan of their music, although I've never paid attention to their lyrics, really, so maybe I should and see if I have more rage for technology than I already do. Doubtful.

My disdain is large. I wouldn't mind the Internet going down if no one got hurt–or if less people got hurt than get hurt now. Did you know that the letter W in English is the letter for the number six in Hebrew? So that would make WWW equal to 666. And yes, I have the mark. I think everyone I know does except for infants and the Amish. Oh, and Orthodox Jews. And some Muslims and probably every other religion in the world. I'm sure there are Hindu yogis without smartphones. And definitely there must be monks without them.

Everclear is playing now. Reminds me of liquor and that time I saw them at Music Midtown in Atlanta. Greer was there. Well, that is her middle name, but she probably wouldn't care if I used it. She used to tag walls with that name. Oh yeah, I've decided to use people's real names based on whether or not I care.

Father of mine. His real name is Bobby. If you look up the gematria of his full name in Hebrew in Euler's number, you'll find that the preceding digits of that position is the zip code of our hometown. I have to mention his real name because of Tori Amos. For a while I thought a lot of her songs were about me. I sent her a letter because my friend worked at the theater in Chicago she was playing at. Our friends are friends. I think she read it but was probably freaked out by some of the facts I told her. It kind of freaks me out, too, though.

I'm Still Alive by Pearl Jam is now on. Yes, I am still alive, and I'd like to keep it that way (without torture) for as long as possible, I guess. I don't know. Be careful what you wish for. Ugh. Skipping song.

I don't feel like listening to STP. Actually I like this song. I definitely have at least one hole in my spiritual heart. I'm not sure about my physical one. I think I would know if I did. My good friend Brandyn died the other day. He had heart problems. He was a good guy, even though I call him her a lot because that's what I was used to him as. I'm not sure if people are as hung up on gender after they die. Pretty sure they wouldn't be.

I was briefly friends with Alexis Arquette, a famous trans actress. My boyfriend went missing once, and Alexis wouldn't help me find him, and she called me a hipster. So I called her Robert and blocked her. But then she died. My friend Paul told me about it. Paul is cool. Oh, point being, I went to People Magazine to read about it, and it said that some of her last words were that she had seen through the veil to a world where there was only one gender. That sounds nice. But then by the time I showed my mom, they had changed the article for some reason. That was weird.

Paul sold Moby's soul on eBay once. They were best friends. Paul was on David Letterman once. I think it was the time he had the inverse mo-hawk. He really likes photo booths and making movies. His movies are weird. We get vegan cupcakes together sometimes. He has a dog. I hope his dog is still okay. I should ask him about her. He has a wife, too, but I don't know her. I can't remember if he had a human child. I doubt it. He's vegan.

I guess I inadvertently ended up talking about the 90s, even though our paths hadn't crossed then.

And now Tori Amos. I could write a whole book attached to thoughts about Tori Amos alone. I wonder who the muses are. Freaky thought. That makes me want a cigarette. Seems like we got a cheaper feel now. She's putting on her stringbean love. This is not really, this is not really happening. You bet your life it is.

Randall's nickname for me was stringbean. He was going to get a tattoo of a stringbean before he died. He got a mixed tape with Greer written on it. We both had the same flame tattoos, except his was on his chest, and mine is on my stomach. Rabbit, where'd you put the keys, girl?

Mmm Mmm Mmm Mmmm. I wish my hair would turn to bright white, but I don't want anyone to smash me. God shuffled his feet.

I have visions. I was in them. I was looking into the mirror. Ugh. I identify with this song a lot. That's probably not entirely true at all points in my life, but it's definitely like me a lot. I don't want to lose my legs, although it would probably do me well. Let's compromise and find a nice Mediterranean environment for me. I could still work. Is piercing your tongue kosher? So many questions.

I asked Facebook if anyone would be interested in reading my book and helping me name chapters and censor myself. And I definitely need an editor because I hate reading books. This Freewrite doesn't have arrow keys, which is a good thing. I'm glad. I need to focus on writing.

Pearl Jam is starting to get on my nerves. I'm sorry. The Breeders are on now. That's more like it. I love her so much. Kim Deal. She's cool. I would like to hang out with Kim Deal as long as she doesn't try to hurt or or no one tries to hurt us because of it, you know. She knows I'm a real coo-coo. Actually, that would be extremely weird if she knew me. I highly doubt she knows me. You never know, though. We probably know some of the same people. I'm sure there's probably no more than 3 degrees of separation. It'd probably be through Courtney Love. Maybe not. I can't think of who she would hang out with. I have no idea, really. Bjork, maybe. She used to babysit this really cute guy I knew in Brooklyn. I rented his room for a while. He was so fucking cute. Oh, my god. So cute. I wonder what happened to him. Kari was his name. I'm pretty sure I have the Bjork story right. Sometimes I get people and stories mixed up. But it's usually not off by very much.

The Lemonheads were giving me a headache, so now The Presidents of the United States of America are playing. Peaches, of course, remind me of home. But it also reminds me of my first and only girlfriend, Susan. Her IRC name was Peaches. She sold elevators for a while, but now she lives in London, I think. I could never get it up for her because I was gay and all. But we used to make out to Matchbox 20. Well, we did once, at least.

Yay, my friend Bryan will help me censor this. So that might not always be his name. Bryan, I need you for this. Be my moral compass!

Okay, I was going to stop writing for the night and let everyone read what I've already written, but I got stuck in a negative space in my head. I accidentally–sort of–sent a message to a bunch of people that were either dead or not my friend anymore on Facebook Messenger. It was in a group. I meant to only send it to Alli.

Anyway, Lane read it. He likes it. I trust his taste. He once called me a no-talent fuck. He used to live with me at The Farm. Fuck I miss Cheri. She was so awesome. Oh shit, I'm supposed to change their names. I'll just have someone else do it before I publish this, that is–if I can work up the courage to do it. There's just so much you don't know about me and my life and my brain and... I'm just really fucking fucked up. Fuckered up, really. I'd say it's the weed, but that's only part of it.

Scott accepted his invitation. I'm wondering if he'll really read it. I love him dearly, but I can't really see him reading a whole book. Well, maybe he'd read a fantasy novel or something. I don't know why I can't picture that. In a bath. As a dog. With a martini in one hand and a Kindle in the other. Dark Purple and magenta in the background with a hint of scarlet. Over the mountains. Smoking a cigar.

Scott was at The Farm, too. I'm not entirely sure what he would want me to refrain from mentioning. Maybe letting people read this was a bad idea. I mean, okay, one time he was really, really drunk and wanted to cuddle basically, although there may have been some penis involved. Sorry, Scott, you can have an alias. How about Professor Chumbypants. Now I feel bad. Editor, please make this change.

It will all be better once the names are changed. The names are changed. I need music. That's the problem. What should I listen to next? Fuck it, more '90s Alternative.

This is going to be a very unconventional book. I just hope I won't regret it. Porno for Pyros are on. I never listened to them much, but they're not too bad. I identify with their name. The guitar is just a little too squirrely or something.

Next. Gin Blossoms. I used to mow the lawn to this album when I was a kid. I miss being a kid. I want to time travel and be back in my 1997 body or something. Any earlier would be too weird. I need a cigarette. Until I hear it from you.

Oh shit I just remembered to ask for Chantel's e-mail address. By the way, everyone can edit this if they want. It is a community effort if you want it to be. I really don't know if anyone would want it to be. Is that a good idea? I mean, some people–for sure. But I need to be selective. For now. Until it gets edited. Maybe this is a bad idea. Pearl Jam is on again. Fuck. This has nothing to do with Art, by the way. Or art. Is this art? What is art considered in the literary world? There are so many worlds. Tori is friends with Neil Gaiman, who is a literary guy. And Neil is friends with my friend Craig. Craig is crazy, too. But we're cool and crazy. I think I'm way crazier than him, but he draws cartoons so he's cooler.

Lane is friends with Craig, too. I think Bryan may be, too. I don't know. How is everyone connected? I think Chantel and Bryan know each other. And Shannon. Shannon wanted to read.

Her mom was a cop. They're both cool. I literally have nothing negative to say about any of them.

Red Hot Chili Peppers. I don't really want to listen to them, but I was there on the boardwalk when they filmed a music video. I gave a security guard a letter to give them, but who knows what was even in it. I think it was during the time I was trying to promote the Music Instrument Library. Damn, I have so many people to write about. I've known a lot of people.

Chantel has helped me a lot before when I was super crazy. She is very nice. And fun. I miss hanging out and drinking and listening to music a lot. Those were good days. They don't have to be over. Shannon would come over to Fern's sometime, too. Damn, we used to have good parties. And Lila and Clift. Maybe I shouldn't be using everyone's real names. I don't know. This is extremely frustrating. Who needs chapters, anyway?

Adelaide just texted me. She just asked if I wanted to come watch Season 4, Episode 13 of The Magicians. It's either my first or second favorite episode. So I'm definitely doing that right about now. Applause.

Well, that was good. I didn't cry. I think I've watched the scene where Quentin dies. Sorry, spoilers. Nicole says I remind her of him. Or vice versa. I can absolutely see it. I just wish I had his hair.

I wouldn't mind going on a date with Elliot, as long as he's single. I'm assuming he's at least bi. I haven't had good sex in a long time. I need to work on myself first, though. For sure. Like my teeth. I need new teeth. I could go without new hair, but I wouldn't mind some. I also need to lose maybe twenty pounds.

I'm back to listening to '90s Alternative. I've met my daily quota of words, but I don't want to stop typing. I just have so much in my head at any given moment that it's nice to put it down on paper–well, e-paper. I think this may be the best invention ever made. I just hope nothing bad comes from it that would be worse than the bads that would come from not doing it. You know?

Adelaide thinks I should only allow people to comment, but I think I'm just going to write the whole book first, let maybe one person edit it, and go from there. Maybe this will be a scroll–scroll-format, at least. I don't know how to divide it into chapters. But what if people get annoyed by not having chapters? Everyone's so addicted to modern technology, though, and people do love scrolling as long as they can pick up where they left off.

Candlebox is playing now. This really reminds me of the 90s–specifically Greer and Randall and Lilly and Kriete and Fern and Nicole and all kinds of other people. Holly. Becky. Mandy. So many people. So fucking many people. Holy shit I have a lot of people in my head. I've loved a lot. I've hated a lot, too. And I've been hated a lot. But there's been a lot of love. Some say the two are connected.

I have a lot of anxiety right now. Oh, I told Adelaide that this was going to be a traumedy meta-novel. So there's that.

Lane said it seemed like I was going to tell longer stories at some point. I have so many long stories to tell. This is really one giant long story. But my psyche is a bit fractured. I think that's what she called it–the director of a psych ward I was at in Atlanta. I got kicked out of the program for hooking up with my 19 year old Muslim roommate. That's kind of a long story. He had a freckle on his dick. All I did was give him a blowjob, but I couldn't keep my mouth shut. I was upset because he stopped giving me attention, including sitting with me at lunch, so I got upset and told them I wanted to leave. And they asked why, so I told them. But then he called the cops and alleged that I raped him. Of course I didn't, and they knew better. It sucks to be falsely accused.

I did have a habit when I was younger to feel up straight guys when we were really drunk. But they all know about it. Once I wasn't completely sure if my friend was sleeping. I later asked him about it, and he said he was. He hasn't spoken to me since. I was just testing the waters, although I know in this day and age, there is no excuse according to most people. That's probably the worst thing I have ever done.

Primitive Radio Gods. I love this song so fucking much. Do do do do do do. My entire being hurts. Oh, I once thought I was the reincarnation of King David. I had evidence and all. Still do. That's a long story I could tell. And I will. But I'm not going to pressure myself. This can be as long as I want it to be.

I've been down-hearted, baby.

I should definitely start changing names in case I have to be my own editor. Gwen Stefani is singing. Well, No Doubt. Maybe it's okay to mention famous people. I told Alix I thought that there was a law here protecting writing about public figures. But what about public figures' private lives? Would that be legal? Also, I don't want anyone to want to hurt me, as I have said numerous times already. I'll try to stop saying that.

It's all ending. We've got to stop pretending who we are.

Do we? Should I? Am I? Who am I really? That is the question of the lifetime. How am I not myself? I need an existential detective. If one even exists, I doubt I could afford to hire them. And I doubt my mom would allocate the money for such an endeavor.

My name is **REDACTED** No, I can't do it. Please edit that. My name is Jupiter Davidson. I was born **REDACTED** in **REDACTED** to **REDACTED**. No, definitely not. Should the names and places be changed to protect the guilty? Guilty according to whom? In the sun, in the sun I feel as one. In the sun. In the sun. Married? Buried?

Kurt Cobain. Yva said that he would have made out with me at a party. I totally would've made out with him. It's a shame he's dead. It's a shame a lot of people are dead. Choking on the ashes of our enemies. Yva kicked me out in the middle of the night and took her hat back all because I brought up an article about how there was a higher percentage of freed black people who owned slaves than white people. She said I was racist. She said Krist Novoselic was racist, too. That's why they broke up.

I'd like to talk to him and get his take on it all. Who knows. I don't think I'm that racist. I definitely know people who are much more racist–of all colors. Colours. That makes me think of Canada.

So I might have a secret. A big secret. But I'm not sure if I'm going to tell you. It depends. If I told you, then millions of people would probably read this. I don't know if I want everyone to know, though. Mainly, I don't know how this book is going to go. So far it has been completely non-fiction.

Okay, I was going to tell you that I'm secretly a member of Brakebills, but that doesn't sound very believable, unfortunately. I could be a Greek God, although that is clearly megalomaniacal.

I love Live. I used to swoon over Ed. I don't know how to spell his last name. This reminds me of Canada, too. Am I babbling? My back hurts. I bought a bottle of wine that I forgot about until just now. It's some fancy French wine with sulfites. Jodot or something. Je ne sais pas parler français. Is that right? Last night my ex-boyfriend told me that I have too much anxiety. He's probably right. He has a stutter and reminds me of Moses for some reason. I love him. I have a photograph of him somewhere with Snuggles and me.

I feel so goddamn old. I am getting old. I'm definitely old to some people. I'm like two generations removed from the up-and-coming generation. That's more than one. That's a lot. They say that I am a Xennial. That word has numerous connotations, but it sounds nice. I think I might take another hot shower. That was nice. And I have to pee. BRB.

Well, the shower was nice, but now I'm freezing. Listening to In the Morning of the Magicians by The Flaming Lips. It came on while I was in the shower (on Spotify from my mark of the beast). I think I may have lost the will to type. My high has worn off, too. I think it was the shower. I wrote a song once that some people liked. One of the lines was talking about never wanting fame or fortune.

I've never really wanted fortune

I've steered far away from fame

I've wandered down most every road

And found they're all the same

I don't feel like typing the whole thing, but you get the picture. My mom just sent me this really sweet meme on Facebook. She told me I should write a book. She didn't say anything else about the matter. Eric's half-brother told me I should write 25k words per at least. I think that's reasonable. Eric's step-dad was Dr. Roberts, who invented the personal computer and was Bill Gates's boss. I had a vision about Bill Gates that came true, but I'm not sure if I should write about it or not. I need to find something chill to watch. I was watching Dirk Gently, but it started jumping the shark a bit. The first season was awesome, though. Elijah Wood and the British guy are so freaking cute. I want dates with them, too, if they're single and heteroflexible at least.

A huge part of me wants to masturbate now, but I'll try to find something else to do. Did you know that it is a common belief in Judaism that Hell only lasts for up to one year? They only pray for people for eleven months, though, not to insinuate someone would be that evil. I need another cigarette. And some wine. Wine reminds me of Alli and the time her husband asked if I was homeless when we were at this fancy bar in West Hollywood. I think I saw Liz Taylor there once. Oh, the night with Alli was the night we sat beside the Australian lady who does hair. Blonde, kind of pointy face, really nice. Pretty.

What should I watch? Please reply. No, that would be weird. Nevermind. I have three cigarettes left. Bummer. Maybe I should take the little piece of Suboxone I have left. Oh, the wine. The wine. It's all the way downstairs, though. I don't even know if there is a corkscrew anywhere. Maybe I should save it for tomorrow. My mind is filled with ideas. To the brim. I need more music. Something different, though. It was a tie between Sadcore Hibernation and Leonard Cohen's You Want it Darker album. They're basically the same.

There's this band called Spokane playing. It was produced in 2000. Good year. Great year. New Year's Eve. Reminds me of that. That was when I met my ex-boyfriend Russell. Moses. Moses. That's his name. Moses.

Greer, Randall, and I went to Hot Topic at the Macon Mall. There was this really cute guy there playing with a fluffy pencil across the display from me. We were checking each other out. He was so cute. Then I got on ICQ and was invited to Justin Bush's New Year's Eve party (1999 to 2000). I go there with this guy Joe, I think. He stepped on a slug. He was my date, but I ended up holding hands under the blanket with Moses. And we danced to Amazed by Aerosmith. Justin, his boyfriend, was really sweet. He was also a porn star. Justin ended up dying years later from HIV. We hooked up a few times. I remember once he asked me if he was a good bottom. He was. He was sweet.

I never got HIV, but I've had HPV, Syphilis, and the clap, I think–whichever one causes your peepee to feel like it's pissing razor blades. Horrible. Sorry famous people I think are cute. Cat Power is playing now. I love them. And I love cats. Power is okay, I guess, although I have never had very much–well, maybe the power of seduction when I was younger. That would explain all the STDs.

Castles and Caves. Lightning Dust. This is really, really good. I'm a little mesmerized. 2007. That was the year I was working at The Base. I loved that job. I had a good life then. Even Nicole said she used to see me riding around town and would think, "Hey, Ben's got his shit together". Fuck, I mean Jupiter. Oh, well. This song is so fucking good. For real. Listen to this if you want to know how I feel right now. I just shared it on Facebook. No one will really understand. Oh well. It's pretty dark here in this tunnel. Haunting the night.

I just remembered Myndi wanted to read, so she's the last person I'll be adding. She's good friends with Kira. We all went to this weird bar once in Long Beach or something. And I had a street hotdog (you know, the kind the Mexicans make with peppers and mayonnaise). Oh, we went to this other bar in Los Feliz or Echo Park or something, I think. They had a photobooth. I got so drunk, as I usually do. Maybe I should have that glass of wine now. Or should I wait until tomorrow?

The music went off. But I turned it back on, and I feel better. I just need to focus on the music. I want a nice cute guy to cuddle with. That'd make me feel better. Or a Xanax, maybe. I just need something. I really do. The Suboxone tastes so bad, though. Once I ate one at my rich Jewish friend's house and pretended to be a spider. That was fun. Yeah.

I'm watching The Mountain Goats play a live show that they did earlier today. I'm thinking about getting a greyhound ticket tomorrow and going back to Georgia for a while. Maybe Florida, too. I feel like I need to move my energy while I'm writing this. Maybe I should go to Short Mountain for a bit, if they'd have me. The last time I was there was during the solar eclipse. I stayed in the goat barn. I had a pretty intense time. It was a pagan sanctuary. Radical faeries. Beautiful place. Interesting people. I'm a little nervous about writing what happened there. But I probably should.

I'm almost out of cigarettes, though. Maybe this should wait until tomorrow. I don't know. John is talking about a conspiracy involving the Gates Foundation. He's joking, though, I guess. Who knows? Let me see how much tickets are.

I could go from Louisville to Macon for $116 on April Fool's Day. Or I could fly for $153 plus baggage fees. I think I'll take the bus. Or does this make me a fool? Should I stay? I don't know.

I'll ask Adelaide what she thinks tomorrow. Just stay alive. Wow, John Darnielle has a son. He's such a family man. Our worlds are probably vastly different, but I identify with some of his music. I'll call my mom tomorrow to see what she thinks. Or maybe now, even though it's 12:43 AM.

My mom thinks I'm putting too much pressure on where I need to be. She just wants me to go back to school. And she wants me to stay put for a while, at least until I get vaccinated. She says to think on it for a day or two, because I always jump to conclusions. I may feel differently, or I may not. I'll ask Adelaide. I really want a glass of wine, but I have one cigarette left after this one. Tomorrow, tomorrow. I've already written almost 8,332 words today–well, more, actually, since I do backspace occasionally.

The kitty is on my bed. Yay! I love this kitty. His name is Itchy. He's solid black and really sweet, even though he pees on Adelaide's pillow sometimes. She thinks it might be because she had his balls removed. I wonder if he would be sad if I left. I wonder if my cat Cupcake misses me. I know I miss her.

I have an awful feeling, and I'm not really sleepy at all. Goddamnit, I'm getting a glass of wine. Fuck it.

Nevermind. I don't think there's a bottle opener. Also, it's getting cold in my room, and the fan on the heater stopped working. I should probably unplug it before I burn the house down. I want someone to hold me. One time they had me strapped down in the back of an ambulance and strung out on Ativan. That was comfy.

Maybe I should just masturbate. I started to look at porn, but I started thinking about Jesus and stuff or something. I feel like I've gotten a couple signs that I shouldn't ejaculate. One was a literal sign. My little niece had left one in the upstairs window of my parent's house while I was in the backyard contemplating the morality or theological implications of masturbating. The sign read "No coming in and out" (it was her playschool room).

But only the words "No coming" were visible. I really, really need a relief, though.

I hurt. Or crying would be nice, too. But it'd be easier to cum than to cry. Maybe I'll use my imagination. It usually goes toward my friend Opey's giant dick. That's his stage name. I'm not sure if he would care if I mentioned him. He is happily married with several kids now. I always used to have straight guys who would bend for me. I've wondered if I'm trans. I've definitely fantasized about being a woman many, many times. I wish I could just take a pill and magically be a genetic female. Did I mention how supposedly homosexuals can reincarnate into women? That'd be nice, maybe. Maybe not. I don't know. I'm already barren. I'm really not a size queen, I swear. It's just a fetish, I guess.

I feel so lonely or something. Maybe I should call my ex. Moses. We never really have sex anymore when we see each other, but I love him. And I think he loves me. Maybe I should listen to something different.

I have a slight urge to cut myself, even though I'm not a cutter. I've only really cut once. I still have a scar. It was with a small screwdriver on my wrist. I did it the right way, but I missed the vein. All because of a boy. Paul. The Republican. I catfished him on Craigslist to catch him cheating. It worked. He used to work for Tucker Carlson, the guy with the bowtie. I wonder how many guys have broken my heart?

My eyes are starting to burn a little. Go down to the Netherworld. Head on down, and plant grapes.

He raised $2,382. Good for him. Oh, he raised it for the Native American Heritage Association. That's really good. I used to live on Pine Ridge Reservation, the poorest place in the country and geographic pole of inaccessibility. John Badwound told me that he was trying to bring back traditional values on the rez. The suicide rate among teenagers is really high, and a lot of people are on meth. Allegedly Catholics used to kidnap the children, cut their hair, and force them into their schools. Supposedly the found bones of the children underneath one of the schools. I've met some nice Catholics, though. I don't think they're all kiddie killers. That's still fucking fucked up, though.

I really need to try to get some sleep. Maybe I should put on a movie. How about a 90s movie? Nevermind. I think that would make me feel lonelier.

CHAPTER III

Adelaide is using the bathroom, and then we're going to Subway. I fell asleep watching Golden Girls last night, and when I woke up it was still on. I love that show so much. I think I'm going to eat cheese on my sandwich. I feel like that verse is misinterpreted. It just says you shouldn't eat a kid with its mother's milk. It doesn't say you shouldn't eat meat and cheese together at all. Although upon closer inspection of Genesis, it does seem that vegetarianism is preferred. Keeping kosher is hard.

Adelaide just had a bowel movement, but she doesn't want anyone to know. She says she heard it's supposed to be in the shape of a banana and float, but hers doesn't float. I wonder if she knows that I'm writing about it. Maybe, maybe not. I don't think she would care too terribly much. Nevermind, she said she knew I would do that to her.

She's changing right now. I've seen her boobs hundreds of times. She's a very beautiful woman, but I feel absolutely zero sexual attraction, unfortunately.

Okay, we went to Subway in Carefree. I got a pack of Chesterfield Menthol 100s, a Cold Cut Trio with mayo and lettuce (American Cheese and Italian bread), and a bag of Cheddar & Sour Cream Ruffles. I ate maybe a quarter of the sandwich. It was okay.

Adelaide's going to help the 92 year old that takes care of use the bathroom. She's a trooper. I wouldn't really want to facilitate in something like that. Other people's bodily ejections make me gag.

Oh, she gave me a Stacker energy pill. We'll see how that goes. I'm hoping I'll be able to procure a corkscrew at some point. The Magicians is paused while she's gone. I think I'll have a smoke. By the way, I woke up feeling really awkward about what all I wrote last night while I was high. I don't remember if I mentioned that already.

I just had a difficult poop. It's probably because I haven't had any Suboxone in a couple days. That happens. I feel slightly okay, though. I know that's too much information. Do I babble too much? I think I might babble too much. Babble on in Babylon. I could go many places with that. I really wouldn't mind a Lortab or something. That'd be nice. I'm such a fucking junkie. Did I mention I've been to rehab several times? That brings a flood of memories, too. My fingers are fast, but not nearly as fast as my recollection. Sad.

I just took off my beanie and looked in the mirror. I kind of look hot in this lighting, even though my head is missing a lot of hair. I'd do me. Well, I'd mutually masturbate with myself, at least. Oh, yeah, I ended up getting off last night while thinking about Opey. Is that weird? I always feel kind of gross afterwards. I have a really old picture of his penis in my Google Drive, but I only really open it up to show people how big it is.

I should go visit him when I'm back in Georgia. The last time I hung out with him I was pretty crazy and didn't have an amazing time, but I think the time before was my birthday. That was nice. I fell asleep in his bed, and he and his wife woke me up with a tray of breakfast food and a cup of coffee. I was delighted, and even more so when I realized there was a Lortab sitting on the napkin. Great people. He wants to be a woman. I mean, he wouldn't mind being reincarnated as a woman or something. I can't imagine him getting his peepee chopped off, though. That would be tragic.

There's a picture of Adelaide's grandmother sitting on her shelf. She looks really pretty and happy and young. She died when Adelaide's mother was fourteen. She found her covered in blood. That's all I really know. Adelaide's mother died when she was fourteen, too. She's worried, I think, that she'll die when her daughter is fourteen. She still lives in Georgia, though. Apparently her step-mother is pretty cool. I hope she doesn't die young.

I need some music and something for the pain. My whole body hurts. I've had a few doctors and friends tell me that they think I might have fibromyalgia. My mom has it. So does Nicole. I tried to call Nicole while I was smoking because I wanted to know what alias she wanted me to use for her, but she didn't answer. She yelled at me the other day for asking too many questions, but then she apologized and said it was because her mouth was hurting. I completely understand that.

Okay, I need another cigarette. I'm a chain-smoking son of a bitch. Or I just have way too much anxiety. Or both. I really kind of want to quit, but I don't have enough motivation, apparently. They should just ban cigarettes. That's the only way I'll be able to quit permanently, probably. I like them entirely too much.

That reminds me of the time I went super crazy and thought they were poisoning the American Spirits I'd buy at the Circle K in Cochran. Actually I think it may have been Flash Foods back then. I kept smoking them anyway because I'm a fucking addict.

So I took a quarter of a Suboxone. You're supposed to let it dissolve in your mouth, but I puked in my mouth like three times and finally had to chase it down with some Coke. Such a horrible taste–second only to burnt meth. I wish I could just be okay without any substances. I don't know how to do that, though.

This large dog is sniffing my Freewrite. He looks kind of sad. I wonder why. Maybe it's because Adelaide is gone. I'd give him lots of pets, but he smells really bad. He needs a bath. We got some dog shampoo at Walmart last night. I was going to give him a bath the other day. I tried to coax him into the bathtub, but he didn't seem too enthusiastic.

I scratched his head some. Now there are hairs on my screen. He smells so bad. He's all up in my face sniffing me now. He licked my hands while I was trying to type. I think he thinks he's a puppy, even though he probably weighs more than me. Thankfully he knows how to get down when you tell him to. His name is Samson.

I wonder if anyone would be interested in publishing this insanity. Maybe then I could make some money and write from the point of view of a rich person. I'd get my teeth fixed first. I went to the dentist the other day, and it's going to cost a ridiculous amount of money, which I do not have. I only have $2000 worth of insurance per year. That's more than most, though, probably. Thankfully the government thinks or knows that I am too crazy to hold down a job. Maybe my job is being a writer. Adelaide thinks I'm an ambassador from another world. Maybe she's right. I just want to throw a big party with all of my old friends.

That reminds me of the song I wrote that I quoted from a while back:

And if reincarnation is what we have in store,

I hope we all meet wasted on a great big dance floor.

And when the DJ plays our song, our eyes will open wide.

We'll see each other as we were, and take back our goodbyes.

I know that's not the way they say the story goes,

But if I were a betting man, I'd double down on "nobody knows".

I almost bought a scratch-off when we were at the Pilot, but Adelaide was coming out of the store right as I was about to go in, and she said "let's go", so I went. I've never bought a scratch-off in Indiana before. I used to have an addiction when I was younger. My dad is a disabled Vietnam veteran, so I got almost $1000 per month to go to school. I'd blow almost all of it on tickets, and I'd buy more with my winnings, so I never really won anything. It really is an addiction. I have a ridiculously addictive personality. I need another cigarette. Goddamn. Sorry, God, although I don't think that's what taking the name in vain means.

Adelaide just got naked again. She invited me to go eat steak with her and Timmy. I asked her if it was a date night, and she didn't know. She said they won't be making out or anything, although he is her lover. She's old enough to be his mother, by the way. I don't think there's anything wrong with that, though. I find myself attracted to younger people, too, although I'm not sure if I would date one. She got excited when I told her she was a main character in my book. Then she belched. Now she's brushing the hay out of her hair from when she was feeding the horses and rabbits. Gerry, this retired stud, has been feeling ill lately. Apparently he's been having a lot of erections, too. I think he just needs a girlfriend.

Now she's blasting Cardi B in the shower. I think that's who it is, at least. It's not typically the kind of music I listen to, but whatever floats your little man on the boat. "It's fucking cold. Goddamn!", she exclaims. That might be because I took another hot shower while she was gone. I was just feeling very dysphoric. I feel better now. It could be because of the Suboxone, but allegedly it only works if you let it dissolve in your mouth, and I swallowed it.

I need a nicotine drip or something. I have some patches in my backpack, I think, but I never think to wear it. I also have some nicotine gum in my pocket. Cigarettes are disgusting, but they are also a part of me. Nicole, Greer, and I were going to quit. But Greer said that cigarettes were all she had left. That's pretty sad.

Greer has been one of my best friends since high school. I vividly remember the first day I talked to her. She was sitting alone wearing a blue plaid shirt with her hair over her face outside at the concrete picnic tables in high school. We didn't really like each other at first. Or rather, she didn't like me. She taught me to stand up for myself more. She has the flame tattoo, too, I think, although she never shows hers. We got them on the same day. It was done with a needle with thread wrapped around it dipped in gel pen ink. We got it because we were obsessed with the movie Foxfire.

I ended up meeting Jenny Lewis, who played Red, when I was at her Rilo Kiley show. I showed her my tattoo, and she thought it was weird. She bummed a cigarette from me, and I picked up the butt when she wasn't looking. **REDACTED** still has it in a little plastic see-through case. I mean Greer.

Greer had gone with me to Los Angeles after I left my job at The Base. We sublet Paul's butler's apartment in this mansion in the hills. It was absolutely gorgeous. The view was amazing. Greer and I ended up getting kicked out of Rage with Joss Stone after we were caught smoking weed with her. Joss did get my ID back from the bar for me, though. We wanted to go wherever they were going, but we weren't invited. Fame makes things tricky, I think. Although we probably wouldn't have been invited even if she weren't famous. That makes me want another cigarette. Everything is a trigger. That was my nickname when I was at this mindfulness rehab in Palm Desert. Trigger. I have way too many boogers, by the way. This house is oddly dusty. I should start wearing my glasses again, maybe. My niece said they made me look like a professor. That's not a bad look. I've definitely had crushes on professors before. I wrote a song about one of them. That was a disaster. I'm surprised I wasn't banned from school or something.

When I saw you standing there

Rolled cigarette and slicked back hair

I knew our paths would someday cross

I hope it's not a total loss

Maybe I'm just narcissistic

Emotionally masochistic

But I cannot seem to get you

Out of my head, am I in yours too?

I think I got a B in his class. I stopped caring when he told me my behavior wasn't appropriate. I don't even remember his name. He was Italian, though, I think. I wonder how many people he's told about me and how he describes me. Oh, well. Should I go eat steak or not? I wouldn't mind getting out of the house for a bit. I like people-watching a lot. I need to brush my teeth.

I heard this rabbi say–well, a couple rabbis, actually–that a very self-centered person can be reincarnated as a bee so their soul can do something for others. I don't think I'm completely selfish, but maybe I should be a bee for a while. I think the word for bee is pronounced the same as my name in Yiddish or something, but I could be wrong. It also means "I". I could be wrong. Don't quote me on that.

Okay, I guess I'm going to go eat with them, even though the thought of eating meat isn't extremely appealing to me right now. Maybe I'll just have a salad or something–or a very small steak. Meanwhile, I'm going to watch Rick & Morty with Timmy while Adelaide feeds the horses.

We just got back from Texas Roadhouse. Adelaide is livid because Itchy pissed on her pillow again. She keeps saying she's going to murder him, but I know she'll be over it tomorrow. She put his nose in the pillow and sprayed him with water. She's still yelling.

We had to wait almost two hours to be seated at the restaurant. It definitely wasn't worth it. The ranch dressing on my salad was delicious, though. And the croutons were the perfect texture–not too hard, not too soft.

I just ate another THC gummy, so I'll definitely write more when it kicks in. I should probably tell an actual story about my past, since, you know, this is a memoir and all. Memoir or memoirs? I don't know. My friend Mona keeps messaging me on Facebook. His grandfather was the last war chief in the Crow tribe or something. There's a picture of him with Obama. I think I'll visit Montana once and if my camper van is finally fixed. My dad bought it for me after my last real boyfriend died. Oh, yeah, that's something I should probably write about. Meanwhile, we're going to watch another episode of The Magicians. We're on the last season, although this is the third time I've watched it.

Oh my Gods, you guys, I'm really high. And I just went through a hellscape in my head. I don't even want to write about it because I don't want to manifest that shit. Is this the wrath of God? Ha Satan? There is a large dog on the floor. He is much larger than me, I think. But he thinks he is a puppy. I just have paranoid thoughts sometimes. That is all.

There is also a cat by the door. That brings me comfort, even though once I thought my roommate's cat was trying to suck my soul out through my toes because I accidentally made a deal with her. But I was high, and it was annulled at the last moment when I couldn't handle the feeling. I definitely need to change all the names so no one wants to exercise me. I'm not entirely sure how to spell that word. Thank you, spellcheck. Should I spell check? Is spellcheck passe? Would grammar snobs even like my book? I don't really read books anymore.

My first favorite book was called The Ancient One. It was about a little girl who time traveled through a tree to fight the logging industry or something. Don't quote me on that. It was really large. The book. Like .. well, you know. I smoke too much. Polar bears are awesome.

Larkin just asked me if I ever got to meet the rabbi, and he wants to know what he said. I can't really remember at the moment. I am pretty high. I'm terrible with remembering dialogue except during possibly intense moments, but even then allegedly I remember it wrong. Can I still be sued if I'm mentally disabled? I don't want anyone (person, corporeal or incorporeal) to hurt me.

I don't want any animals at all to hurt me. Bugs can eat me when I die. I used to want to be set out in the woods so wild animals could eat me. I should definitely publish under a pseudonym if I publish at all. I really, really, really don't want to be famous. I want to live somewhere safe where no one will hurt me. Maybe I should be vegan.

I need to talk to someone on the phone. I'm trying to call Moses, but he's not answering. I'd call Jesus if I knew his number. I could call his brother.

I talked to Franco, Jesus's brother, for a while. He said I could use his real name. I thought he was God once. I stole my disability check from my mom, cashed it, and bought several roxys and a hotel room. Greer came and hung out, and after she left I was feeling really, really bad. I begged God for a sign or something, and the phone rang immediately. I asked who it was, and they said, "God". So I really thought that Franco was God for a while. I lost my Converse while walking through a swamp on the way to his house. I was so happy to be there. But then a while later, I was reading the Psalms of David, and a voice in my ear (the first and only time I've had an auditory hallucination) said, in Franco's voice, "Ohhh, you just sold your soul to the devil." I shit you not. Fuck. Now I'm hearing strange noises coming from outside the house, and the dogs next door are barking. I need a cigarette, for sure.

According to Freewrite, I've written just over an hour's worth of material to be read (according to whose reality, I do not know). Dare I share it with others? That's about the same amount of time as a TV show.

Fuck. Adelaide said not to show anyone yet. I've got to do other stuff first or something. I probably need a lawyer. I'll definitely need an editor. Everyone needs an editor. That is a song. By Death Cab for Cutie. I'm going to listen to it now. Wait, no it was Mates of State. I've seen both of those guys before. Mates of State are so cute and looked so in love. The guys from DCFC are nice and probably invited us to their hotel room because Naomi was hot. Naomi wanted to marry me once I think. Or she was in love with me. But I was a fag. I think I led her on, too. Plus I fooled around with three guys she liked while she was in the room. Well, 2 1/2, maybe. I'd color the sky with you. I'd let you choose the blue.

Did I accidentally sell my soul to the devil somehow? My Only Offer. This is a good song. Lord, help me. Or somebody–any being, assuming they are and were originally one. Or at least will be and once were. Time is confusing. I met a guy named I Am who was going to time travel back to Ancient Rome. This guy I knew who was a famous geneticist and blacklisted in the 70s wrote out the equation for time travel on a bench on the boardwalk–probably somewhere between Windward and Sunset. This was 2011, though. That was when I was homeless. Am I an accidental hipster? Was IRC part of God's master plan to get me to be good at and like typing? I type relatively fast–around 130 wpm, probably. About the same. I think I'm borderline "gifted", although some say IQ tests are racist. Maybe I should go there, maybe I shouldn't. Bryan was going to be my moral compass, but I think that went down the drain. I love Bryan. But should I really let anyone read my book until I'm done with it? Will that spoil it or make it more interesting? Is it interesting? I don't know. I think it is, but I also might be a narcissist.

I feel like I need feedback. Should I wait? Desire. Yes, Mates of State, I am talking about your song. Oh my God, if they read this and didn't hate me, that would be so awesome. I should send them a copy when I'm done since they're in it. Maybe I should make a YouTube commercial or something. Self-promotion sounds funny. Eep! I want a soul mate in the flesh that hangs out with me a lot. Maybe I can find someone this way. Maybe that's what the book should be about. Oh wait, no, it's about writing the book. Is that lame? Self-doubt. Some say it's the devil's tool, but I don't think doubt is always a bad thing, necessarily.

Surfjan Stevens is playing now. His shit is pretty chill, even though the words are whatever. I really like the one about the shadow of the cross. That was good. Was that a cover? I have no idea. Maybe it's a cover.

His voice kind of reminds me of Whit's at this part. I don't know why. Whit is the one who gave me the tattoo on my wrist. I thought he was my soul mate. I think he may have been the only person I've ever said that about. He's from Louisville. He was friends with Yva. That's how I met her. We had a month-long experimental monogamous relationship because he was polyamorous and was going to Brazil for tour. I suck at those, apparently. I was pretty dramatic. He wrote a song about the matter. I have slight ill feelings because he doesn't talk to me anymore, but I still miss him.

Oh, I also thought my neighbor was my soul mate once. I thought he was the literal Jonathan to my David. I thought his dad was King Saul. His dad is a preacher. Jonathan told me had a "vision" of me giving him a blowjob one night as he rubbed his crotch. (He was rubbing his crotch as he was telling me this). I'm telling you, straight guys love me for some reason. I think I might be trans. I don't know. Maybe not.

I just had crazy flashbacks for some reason. I don't even remember what I was saying. Sufjan's voice is so nice. Is that his real name? I know Tori's real name is Myra Ellen. But that's about it. I think Myra Ellen is a beautiful name. I wonder if anyone ever calls her that? I wrote a letter to Queen Elizabeth once. I told her not to be scared because I'm friends with Frankie, who went to school with Harry's wife. I was pretty crazy then. I highly doubt she ever read it. I was telling her about the resonance feelings I was getting. I got it that I should tell her about them.

I need to go get the vape before Adelaide goes to bed. Fuck, she probably is already asleep. It's almost 1 AM. What am I going to do? Oh, she's up. Cool. I got the vape and babbled a lot while she was trying to watch The Magicians. She's on the episode with the

Moon. Why is "the" not capitalized in "the Moon". The Moon. Oh, wait. Yeah. I like it better with a capital T. Am I hungry? I'm not really sure. A picture of a Moon Pie flashed in my mind. RC Cola. Yum. They're both okay. I thought a spider was on my keyboard for a second, but it was just a bit of fuzz. I wonder if a lot of people will be embarrassed for me if they read this. I have 1 1/2 cigarettes left. I keep having ideas about how to fictionalize this book. I don't know if that's a water creature that I'd be jumping or something. Jumping the porpoise. Porpoise. Purpose. You see what I did there? You see it?!? You better goddamn see it, motherfucker. Grr. That felt good. I should be angry more often. It feels nice. It feels really nice. Naomi's sister told me once that I use sex as a weapon. That sounds a little rapey. I already told you the rapiest thing I've done. You decide.

I just asked Opey if he wanted to try to make one of my songs sound better. I kind of hope these names get changed. Can I say I changed the names but leave them the same? I should definitely take out my parents' names. But then I couldn't mention how Tori Amos mentions them by name in her songs. Who are these muses anyway? What are muses? I know that's where the word "music" comes from. What are gods? What is reality? This is a touchy subject.

I wonder if he can make me sound better. Maybe someone else could sing it? Oh my god, I love Sufjan's voice so much. I wonder if he would sing one of my songs. That would be so rad. I just offered him $20 on YouTube for him to do it. I wonder if he'll see it. My songs aren't that bad. Although this guy who I thought was in the Illuminati told me I needed to put hooks in my songs to make money at Short Mountain.

Did I mention how fucking tragic my life has been? Oh yeah, Josh. Josh and I dated seven months. That was the longest relationship I've ever been in. By the way, we did a play about our lives when I was in school last semester, and this was one of my scenes. I had my monologue memorized, but I don't feel like remembering it.

Anyway, Josh was acting really strange one night. I found out he smoked weed, which made him crazy. He had been hospitalized more than me–like multiple times more than me. He was fighting with his dad, and then he wanted to have sex with me. But I was watching Chelsea Handler, and I didn't feel like it. The look on his face was just devastated. Anyway, long story short, I fell asleep, and when I woke up to go outside, he was sitting on the floor with his head between his knees. And his toes were blue. And I tried to wake him up, but he was cold. I couldn't even think of who to call. Finally I called 911. I remember going outside and just screaming and screaming, but no one heard me. Everyone was at church. I really loved him. It was the first time I have ever really unconditionally loved someone I dated, I think. He got on my nerves a lot, but I miss him. He had a bad heart, is what we found out.

But for a while there his parents thought I gave him pills to make him overdose. I never gave him anything, although his parents did. That's not why he died, though. It was his heart. It took months for the coroner's report to come back. That was pretty shittie.

I really hate thinking about that. I hate thinking about all my friends dying, actually. I miss them so fucking much.

Randall's boyfriend's ex kidnapped him from work and shot him in the back going down the interstate. Then he tried to set the house on fire and killed himself. That was pretty fucking horrible. Randall has been my best guy friend since high school. He was more than a friend. He asked me to marry him the year before, but I turned him down because I thought it'd be weird because we were so close that we were like brothers, even though we had hooked up a few times.

Randall was a good guy. I have nothing really bad to say about him at all. I mean, he was a little crazy, but who isn't? I love him so much. This song is nice, although I want to hear something different.

I put on a YouTube playlist I call "roadtrip". Adelaide is talking about a road trip to Georgia in April. I don't know if I can wait that long. I do feel like moving my energy when I think about it. I just had the thought about going to see everyone's graves. That'd be nice.

Sharon Van Etten's cover of Flaming Lips's "Do You Realize?" is playing. I like her a lot. This song reminds me of Ronda. She was my house mother at the rehab in Palm Desert. She is awesome. Gorgeous. I can't remember if I've mentioned her yet. I miss her. She's still alive, though. So that's cool. I think I'm going to eat some of my leftover Subway.

It's weird how I'm typing to someone at another point in spacetime. I really hope to hear from you if you've gotten this far.

I mean, do people really want to hear about the extra crazy shit? It gives me a lot of anxiety to think about it, much less type it. I think I need to get drunk first. We still don't have a corkscrew, and I don't want to taste Jager right now. Sometimes I think people know more than you think they do. That's all I'll say about that right now.

Dance Yrself Clean by LCD Soundsystem is on. I love this song. It makes me feel better. It reminds me of dancing my ass off with Lucy at Michael's. I miss them. I want to go see them. I want to write some there. They are good characters. I think this all would be a good TV show, but I'd want to work with everyone involved to develop the characters. I do know a lot of really cool people. And there's a pretty good chance I'm part of some sort of theological conspiracy. Lucy's grandfather or something was a famous Nazi. Maybe I shouldn't say that. I was everything Hitler hated. Or, I am. I wondered once if I were Hitler's reincarnation since I am gay, I have been interested in both Jehovah Witnesses and Judaism, I'm work-lazy, and my maternal great-great grandfather was possibly a gypsie from Scotland. That's what they call them there. Not Romani. I don't know why. They say they used to claim to come from Egypt, but some say they're really from India.

My DNA is 100% Western European according to AncestryDNA, but my father has 1% Senegalese. I thought that was interesting. But my paternal yDNA is Semitic if you go by the Table of Nations. Actually they discovered both my yDNA haplogroup and mtDNA haplogroup at the Cro-Magnon caves. I forgot what they were called. Something French, maybe.

I'm not entirely sure about reality or history or anything like that. You never really know, do you? Or do you? Maybe some do. I don't really know the answer to that. Florda Cash is playing. So pretty. I'm getting old.

I just e-mailed a literary agent. I think she's Jewish. Her last name sounds Jewish.

I was going to go to bed. I took a hot shower, but I started talking to Thomas online. He's my friend's kid. He wants to read my book and do a book report on it for school, but I told him I didn't think he was old enough. I think he's like 13 or something. You're considered an adult at 13 when you're a Jew, I think. He said his sister is his teacher, and that she's cool. Still. I mean, not that I'm even an adult at 38 years old. What does that even mean, really? I'm definitely not responsible or anything. I told him I'd ask his mom if it's okay. His brother Timmy (different Timmy) is in jail. I love him very much. I also love his mom, Kim. She is great. They are all swell. Their little dog Nellie died, though, which makes me sad. She was a miniature Doberman Pinscher. She was so tiny and fragile. A little ball of love. Aw, Nellie.

I wouldn't mind being a little famous–like, I'd want to be invited to cool parties, but I don't want strangers to recognize me or anything. That'd be perfect. I really hope this literary agent lady emails me back. I think the automated response email said she might get back with you after 4 to 6 weeks, but she doesn't get to respond to everything. I wonder if I should give her a little while or try sending it to other people. By the way, I feel compelled to mention that using "wonder" as a verb doesn't require a question mark at the end. It is a statement. I wonder.

I keep forgetting this is supposed to be my memoirs, so I put on the Time Capsule on Spotify. Young Folks is playing. I suck at whistling. I feel like dancing. I remember that I didn't feel that young when this song came out, but I was. Time is weird. I say that a lot.

I asked this guy I know what he thought about what I sent the literary agent, and he said something about the dangers of "word salad", basically. He just didn't use that phrase. But I like salad. What's wrong with salad if it has a good dressing? The dressing definitely makes it. Maybe I should dress up my book. How does one dress up a book? I could put photographs of attractive people in and on it. That reminds me of an old yearbook I had that did that. That was neat. I like collages.

What if no one likes it, though? How can I find someone who will? I'm sure they exist, but where? I should be able to find them utilizing the beast, right? Thirty Seconds To Mars is on. I've never paid much attention to their music, although Jared Leto is a hottie. I miss My-So-Called-Life. That was one of my favorite TV shows ever. One of my favorite scenes was when they were playing Buffalo Tom's "Late at Night". Ricky signed up for the play, and I think Angela and Jordan held hands or something. Maybe I'm getting episodes mixed up. I also liked it when Rayanne sang the Sesame Street theme song. I've been to Sesame Street. I fixed a bunch of computers for Jim Hinson's daughter once.

That was the year I met Clementine. 2004. She's Cybil Shepherd's daughter. She came and picked me up when my roommate kicked me out, and the next day she took me to Cybil's house. She had no idea I was a huge fan. That was strange. Her assistants were like, "we're going to get rid of that Southern accent." They had me watch for Cybil to come out of her bedroom and down the steps because she was filming a commercial for IBS or something. I never got to talk to her or anything. Did I mention I don't think Clementine likes me much? It's all because she thinks I'm a drama queen. She's the one who pretended to be lesbian. Anyway. No, I like Clementine. I just don't like it when people I used to like don't like me. Wait, have I mentioned her yet? I don't remember. Oh well.

I seriously wish I had a guy in my bed right now. Or even Clementine. If I were straight I would've tried to woo her. I don't want to touch her, but the company would be cool. She kissed Naomi once. She used to date Linda Perry for a while. Linda was friends with Courtney Love. Wasn't I trying to figure out who I was connected to through Courtney Love? My short-term memory is horrible. Actually, all of my memories are pretty horrible. Why the hell am I trying to write my memoirs anyway? Clearly I am insane.

I have a very rare blood type: AB-. Does that make me special? Adelaide's is AB+. We both do seem very different from other people. Maybe there's something to it. The Japanese think there is. I'm pretty stoked that Thomas wants to read my book. My mind was elsewhere, by the way. I just realized not all of my thoughts are connected. I usually start a new paragraph when my train-of-thought breaks, but I didn't just then.

For a while there I was a little leary about being friends with Thomas on Facebook. But kids these days hear all kinds of shit on streaming services that I guess it doesn't matter as much–not that I ever really post anything risque, anyway. I also don't want to look like a pedo or anything. I've never found myself attracted to a kid, although I do find some teenagers hot occasionally. I think I may have mentioned that already. I wonder if I would have been considered a borderline pederast in Ancient Rome, although I wouldn't do anything with them probably unless I were really drunk and they seduced me or something. If a 16 year old seduced me, would that still be considered statuatory rape? That may be the age of consent. I have no idea. I think it's either 15 or 16. Anyway, I would rather date someone similar in age to me. Definitely–well, unless they're different from their age group, I guess. The youngest I've kind of dated was 23 when I was like 37. That's not too bad. Is it really that bad that I find teenagers hot sometimes? They're supposed to be hot. That's when they're fertile. The smell of puberty, though. Gross. No thank you. Okay, I think that's enough about that subject. Pederasty is bad!

The word "pederast" reminds me of my friend Alison. I haven't heard from her in years. We used to hang out at Madison Alley in Dublin. And we'd drink wine on Jamie's front porch. That seems like forever ago. Early 2000s. I feel kind of sad. Is anyone still interested? Will a stranger ever read this? I really wish I had a real fucking cigarette. No one cares about this shit. I don't even care. Fuck.

I found a short in the ashtray. I wish I knew what people would want to know about. I hope no one tries to hurt me for being a pederast. It's only in thought.

Broken Social Scene is on. So good. Park that car. Drop that phone. Sleep on the floor. Dream about me. I wish I were 17 again. That was a good age. The dog is back.

I gave him lots of pets, and he licked my face. He is a good dog, even though he's way too big. I haven't had a dog in a while. I spanked the last dog I had because I was going through withdrawals, and it kept shitting on the floor. That's the worst thing I've ever done in the animal kingdom. When I was little, my dad shot a bird in the field behind our house. He wanted me to finish it off, but I couldn't. I cried. I don't like hurting animals.

I should find something to watch. It's almost four in the morning. I think I'm going to watch YouTube videos about The Magicians. I'm lame. I know. Good night.

CHAPTER IV

It's almost 2:30, and I still haven't gotten out of bed. Daniel just called. He's looking for something to do. I know him from rehab in Valdosta. I told him to go be homeless in Venice Beach, but his girlfriend wants a roof over her head, and a tent doesn't count. I need a shower.

Adelaide is freaking out because one of the animals pooped on the floor. She's about to go feed the horses, and then I might ride with her to run an errand about 45 minutes away. I had that drive, though, because it's really curvy and makes me nauseous. She's doing my laundry. I don't mind doing my own, but she offered. She's always doing something.

My brain just started going to weird places. It landed on Clementine, for some reason–the night I stayed at her apartment. There was a dollar on the floor, which I thought must have been a rich people thing. And I found a Scientology pamphlet with really creepy rules. There are a couple more memories attached to the Scientologists.

My old friend Heather, who I haven't heard from in over a decade, used to live by the Scientology Celebrity Center in Hollywood. She gave me and Pirate Scotty some coke to help her move to a larger room. She was a waitress and an actress, as most people in Hollywood seem to be.

I'm really hungry, but I don't feel like eating anything. Adelaide thinks I just need fluid. I'm out of cigarettes, and this vape isn't really doing it for me. I feel like I need a plot. Lane says that the "narrator" of this book sounds like someone very young who has gathered decades of memories. Is that a good thing or a bad thing or neutral? Adelaide brought me my leftover potato chips. Maybe I should eat some.

I smoked one of Adelaide's dad's Montclair Blacks. They're kind of bitter. I wouldn't mind a menthol version, I think. At least it's a cigarette. Cigarettes are bad. Kids, don't smoke. It's uncool, although it used to be cool when I was a kid. But then the government started banning advertisements that appeal to children. My grandfather died from Emphysema. The only memories I have of him are smoking cigarettes on his front porch with his legs crossed. My parents say I remind them of him. We kind of looked alike too when we were younger. He was handsome. Does that sound vain?

My maternal grandfather was a farmer. He quit smoking after the war. He mostly raised goats, but he had a smattering of other animals, too, including chickens and goats. But goat sales were his passion. I went to one or two when I was little. The auctioneers talk really fast, as most auctioneers do. Once my granddad turned his tractor over into the pond. And a brown recluse bit him once, but he wouldn't go to the hospital. He was pretty hardcore. He was also a Master Mason. I'm not sure if it's too soon to talk about the Masons. That's a pretty intense topic. I'm probably less than a quarter of the way through my book, so I guess I'll wait.

My anxiety is kind of high. I forgot to take my morning medicine, as I usually do. I was doing pretty well for a while when I was in Georgia, but I keep forgetting to take it up here. It's probably because my mom was giving me my meds when I was there. I don't need to end up back in a psychiatric hospital, although some of my best times have been had there.

Lane doesn't think I should let Thomas read this. I asked his mom, and she said she would skim over it first if I wasn't sure. Maybe I should make an age limit on reading this, even though I lost my virginity at fifteen. He's almost fifteen. Kids, if you read this, you should wait until you're married to lose your virginity.

Yeah, I should probably definitely make an age limit. Is eighteen good enough? My moral compass isn't that great, and I haven't heard from Bryan. I feel like people reading this are going to think I'm a creep for admitting to being attracted to teenagers, though. I'm pretty sure it's normal, but the collective opinion has definitely changed in recent years. I wouldn't act on it, though. I don't want to act on it.

I like watching cats. Itchy is eating. He's really into it. I wonder what it's like to be a cat. I pretended to be a cat a couple years ago. My mom would leave the door open so I could come into the room and crawl on the bed like a cat. Is that weird? It didn't last long. I didn't poop in a litter box or anything. Actually, one time my friend's toilet wouldn't flush, so I buried my poop in the litterbox, which was in the bathroom. I didn't know what else to do. I doubt anyone ever noticed. I'm going to smoke another bitter ass cigarette and maybe take another hot shower because I'm a fucking addict.

Nevermind. Adelaide is back from feeding the horses and ready to go. I hope this doesn't suck too bad. The roads or just so damn curvy. I remembered to take my medicine, even though I almost puked trying to swallow the pills. I wonder if that literary agent lady will ever reply to my inquiry. I don't want to offend anyone because of my words, although it's probably inevitable. That reminds me of a really good song Shakira sang in Spanish before she became famous here. Okay, Adelaide's putting on deodorant, and then we'll be hitting the road.

Nick Cave's "Into My Arms" is playing in the truck. I don't think Adelaide likes it too much. I like it though. I saw him once at a carwash in Los Angeles. His face is unmistakable. Oh, I've decided I'm definitely going to have an age limit on this book: for mature audiences only. For sure. Yay, the Pixies are playing now. Velouria.

I got another pack of Chesterfields and a bottle of Mountain Dew for Adelaide at the Indian store in Carefree. We're on the road. It hasn't started to get windey yet. Now she's talking about giving the rabbits apples. Apparently they really love apples.

Alright, I'm starting to get sick. It's so damn curvy. Why couldn't they just cut a straight road? I mean, I know it's a very hilly region and all, but damn. Maybe I'll stop writing for a while before I puke.

A cover of David Bowie's "Ashes to Ashes" just came on. I'm reminded of the many times I've done heroin. The three best times were at 3am in a Bed-Stuy laundromat, in my car with Derek in Macon, and at my house in Boyle Heights. But that time we just snorted the liquid after heating it in the spoon. I didn't shoot up. But shooting up heroin is definitely one of the best feelings I've ever experienced.

When I did it in NYC, I was with this guy Piss. He was so beautiful. I think he was a full-blooded Native American. I'm not sure what tribe. I shared his needle, even though he had Hepatitis C. I didn't get it, although I thought I did at the time. My arm swelled up in these little patches that looked like quilted toilet paper. I was being very self-destructive because I thought Whit broke my heart.

I had been working at this great job in Manhattan, but I flew down to Louisville to hang out with him. I was supposed to play a house show with him, but I got really stoned and fell asleep. When I woke up, he was practicing with one of his former lovers, so I got really jealous and tried to hook up with his neighbor.

When I got back to NYC, I went to the Metro in Williamsburg. I told myself I was going to hook up with the first person who showed interest. I went home with an HIV-positive artist and had sex with him for days. That's how I met Piss. Once, the artist and I got really fucked up on some kind of research chemical that was supposed to simulate Peyote. I think it was called 2c-p or something.

We had crazy sex, and his face morphed into like ten different beings. Then he splashed paint all over a canvas on the floor, and a lot of it got on me. I was in my boxers. Still in our underwear, we took the subway to Manhattan, where a cop questioned me why I was handing out tangerines to sex workers.

They were cleaning the subway station, though, and the chemicals seemed really toxic. I seriously thought I was in a concentration camp or something. It was horrible. When we finally got back to the apartment, I cried in the shower for a long time. That was pretty intense.

But yeah, so I met Piss through the artist. Piss and his friends would steal backpacks from people and sell the contents for heroin. Heroin is both amazing and terrible.

We just drove past a skunk. It smelled like weed. I don't understand why people say skunks smell so bad. They just smell like skunky weed. Adelaide is having a little road rage. We're almost to our destination, though, thankfully. "Today's not the day I want to run into a crackhead", she says as a kid tosses a football that lands close to the truck. We're here. I definitely need a cigarette. Ok, we're on the way back home. That was quick.

We're on the way back home. We stopped by Walmart and Wendy's. This road is making me nauseous. Adelaide is driving really fast. She's on the phone with Timmy, I think. She's driving really fast. It's freaking me out a little bit. I'm ready to be home. Oh, she told me I need to edit the parts out about being attracted to teenagers. She says I should call them "young adults". It's not like I'm trying to get with one or anything, though. Damn she's driving fast.

We're six miles away. I think I'm going to eat a gummy and take a hot shower when we get there. Obviously I'm a little addicted to both, even though the gummies have a tendency to throw me into a pretty mean existential crisis. I'm getting a little sleepy, though. I don't know why. I woke up at like 1 PM.

CHAPTER V

I took a shower and ate three squares of THC-infused milk chocolate because I left my gummies in Adelaide's room last night. It hasn't kicked in yet. I was going to watch The Magicians, but she was hot, and the fan was too cold for me.

I just had this weird feeling of saudade come over me. I love that word. Sometimes it's the only word I can find to describe how I feel. I just have this longing for… something. I don't know what or when or who. I just know that I miss it, and I don't know if I'll ever have it again because I don't even know what it is. I have a lot of good memories, though. I wish this would kick in so I'd have more motivation to write about them. I think I might rest a bit.

I masturbated. I did. I only feel slightly ashamed. I'm watching a The Magicians swag unboxing video. A part of me wants to turn this novel into a time travel adventure or something, but even if I wanted to now, that would've spoiled it. You never know what's really going to happen, though, do you? That's another reason I was thinking about getting a bus ticket. At least it would shake things up a bit.

I'm looking at Spotify. I have several people listed in my friend activity. I should write about them.

Evan is listening to "Girl Like Me" by Black Eyed Peas and Shakira. I was just talking about Shakira. That's pretty weird. I haven't even though about Shakira in years probably. Evan was good friends with my boyfriend who died. I think they went to church together or something, even Josh claimed to be a pagan. They played "Imagine" at his funeral. My mom came. She sat beside me. On the other side sat Ty, our mutual friend. He held my head, even though he had a girlfriend. He confused me. That's another story. The 23 year old I dated was his friend. He was super cute. I mean, maybe we didn't technically date, but we talked and hooked up a few times. I think I might've been his first guy. Music says a lot about us.

Next is Kyle Burgoyne. Scapegoat by Atmosphere. He used to drink and party with us in Dublin back in the day. Cassey, Scott, Haley. At Scott's house. This song is giving me anxiety, although it's probably really profound and about me in a way that makes me seem really dumb right about now if you're familiar with the song. The healthcare system really does suck ass. I've had so many therapists and psychiatrists and hospital stays, but I'm still fucked up. I feel a little pukey.

I just don't feel really super passionate about a lot of my stories, even though that's what I'm really supposed to be writing about. Who's next? Matt Oxley. I'm definitely going to have to change these names, I think. Anyway, it's "I've Got Friends" by Manchester Orchestra. I never listened to them much, but this is really, really good so far. Good taste. Matt is a cool guy. He has fixed my computer before, even though I worked in IT for many years and have been fixing computers since I was a kid.

I used to take things apart a lot. I also read a really old set of encyclopedias. I think they were from the 60s. I drew a picture of penicillin once from it. I also tried to create a plant-human hybrid with my semen when I was like twelve or something. That's pretty weird. It sat on the sink in the bathroom for a long time. Nothing ever grew. I think it got moldy. C'est la vie.

French people freak me out. Should I wait to tell this story, or am I going to freak myself out? I don't really feel like feeling freaked out right now. And it is a subject matter that really freaks me out. Honestly, sometimes Truth is stranger than fiction. Well, at least lower-case truth. I'm still not sure about the capital Truth.

Capital. D.C. Eight grade gifted field trip. Some senator was supposed to meet with us, but I think he overslept. Oh, did I mention Jimmy Carter is my fifth cousin? I found that out recently. I did a report about him in fourth grade. I think I actually wrote a poem about it or something.

Oh, I have this cousin. Well, my mom's first cousin is married to this guy who was a state representative. In elementary school I drew a picture of his house with tennis courts and everything, even though I had never been there before. I don't even think he had tennis courts. I also did a paint-by-numbers and tried to say it was my own creation. That's pretty sketchy for a fourth grader. I was a weird kid, I guess.

Ok, Lila has some weird "Nom Nom" kid's song. This really isn't that bad. I kind of dig it. Parry Gripp. That's who it's by. I apologize for mentioning a kid's song in this fucked up tome. I need a cigarette. Next.

Aww, Franco is listening to The Pointer Sisters "Neutron Dance". This makes me happy. Franco is the one I thought was God that time. Jesus's brother. I'm pretty sure I mentioned that. This song is kind of fitting for that. I should call him. He said I could use his name in my book.

Ok, I talked to God. I mean Franco. That was very un-Jewish of me. Or very Jewish. I'm not really sure. Anyway, That's lame. So I asked Lila about whether or not I should change the names because she's a librarian and reasonable I think. She's a mom. I would definitely never want anyone under the age of whatever age people who play Grand Theft Auto V should be. I think moms should decide what age that is. I mean, I think moms collectively should decide unless there is authority that is for sure from actual God.

I want to love God. I do. I want to serve him, but I am also pretty self-serving. I mainly need to break two addictions: drugs (including cigarettes) and possibly masturbation. I mean, I need to stop spilling my seed. It's just that sometimes it's the only thing I know that might make me feel better. I love you, Franco.

Next.

Lane is next. Ron Gallo, "Young Lady, You're Scaring Me". I've never heard this song before. It's pretty good. I wonder if his marriage is happy. I hope it is.

Okay, back to the teenage thing. I'd just like to say that it was pretty common not so many years ago for twenty-something guys to hook up with or date fifteen year olds. I know it sounds very sketchy now, but it wasn't nearly as sketchy back then. I never did it, though. Although once I was really drunk and passed out at some girl's house, and her fifteen year old son played with my dick. I told my friend the next day. I didn't want anyone to think I was a kiddie diddler, even though you're not completely a kid when you're fifteen. Your brain does continue to develop until you're 23, though. That's a good number. That's the age Alli and I were going to get married if we had still been single. But I ended up being gay. Maybe they should increase the age of everything to 23.

Beth Jenkins is next. She's super cool. We used to party at her house when I lived in Savannah. She was good friends with Adam, who is married to a woman and a youth minister or some shit. Good for him. I wish I could get it up for a vagina. Sorry, I know that is very vulgar. Beth is cool. She has red hair.

I just asked her if she would mind if I used her name. I haven't talked to her in a while, but I have good memories attached to her. I always thought she was super rich. I mean, you had to be either really rich or really good to go to SCAD. I've never seen her art. I've never really been that physically drawn to visual art, though. For a while I thought that making images of any kind were prohibited, including for art. Maybe they are. I don't know. This topic stresses me out. There's a song that reminds me of Beth, but I can't think of it at the moment.

Next.

Well, the next one is my friend who wanted a pseudonym. I'm waiting for her to tell me. Frankie. That's it. Frankie. I told her how many words I've written. Shit, it says my battery is low. Maybe I'll go watch The Magicians some more with Adelaide. I'm going to keep typing until I'm at 19,000 words. Seven more words left. I am done.

I'm currently listening to Curacao by Cal Tjader from Frankie's playlist. It is pretty spunky but chill. I dig it. I think I mentioned her already. She's cool. I'm really, really high. Oh, she likes to get high, too. And she's vegetarian. I have to pee.

Okay, I know this may be hard to follow. But next. I love you, Frankie.

Now it's "How Do You" by the Gnoomes. Lori #1 (I have two Loris in my life, but Lori #1 was there first). She lives in England now but is from the dairy capital of the world or something. Or was it turf? No, I think it was cows. People used to call her a mean thing because of her last name that had to do with cows. I miss her. She's Naomi's sister. Their mom takes me in a lot when I have nowhere to go. Goddamn I'm such a loser. Next.

Oh yeah, Lori is a great singer and is in a cool band with her husband Andy in Bristol. I really hope I can keep their real names in here so they can tell people they're in a famous book. That'd be swell. I was in her wedding. Greer and I were late, though. I think we got lost or something. I don't remember. We had to jump up really high for the picture. I think I might self-publish. For sure. You can't squeeze blood out of a turnip, can you? Maybe I should talk to a lawyer and get an editor. Maybe I can edit myself. I just wish I could keep all the names–well, except for maybe my parents' names. I could always redact some stuff. I just don't really feel like reading my whole book. That's a lot of fucking words. Everyone Needs an Editor. That reminds me of Lori. For sure. We used to go to a lot of concerts together back in the day. Next.

Kate. Kate. Savannah, also. And Pennsylvania. She is a goddess. She likes cats. She apparently likes Boney M. also because I'm currently listening to Rasputin. Boney M. has one of my favorite songs, "Rivers of Babylon". Such an amazing fucking song.It gives me the resonance feelings a lot. Oh, I drew my crazy conspiracy theory shit on a door that's in her parents' basement. It's signed "The King David" in Hebrew because this was during the time that I thought I was the reincarnation of David. I had my reasons.

Oh, and her mom. She is a queen. Ellen. She should be a queen. She needs to be a queen. She's definitely a diva. Although she told me once she wanted to retire to a cabin in the woods. Tom, her husband. Great man. Great scientist. And Nora. Oh, Nora. And Barbara. Barbara is such a cool lady. And Patrick. He redid my flame tattoo. I found it very erotic. Sorry.

Fuck. Lila just messaged me back. Her hubby's in the hospital with Covid. Fuck. I'm sure he'll be okay. That still sucks. My sister and niece had it. So did Nicole. I'm not really sure if I've had it. Next.

Autumn Sanders. I know her from The Hummingbird. Those were some good times. "With Or Without You" by U2. Great song. I'm feeling it.

Wait, Lila said that most people will contact the person being written about and give them the heads up especially if there is something bad about them. And she's a librarian. She says to write the book and once it gets locked up, my publisher will help me sort the legal stuff out. That seems reasonable. Thank you, Lila. Lila is stressed out right now because of Clift. Or Cliff. I always say Clift. She said Cliff. But it could've been auto-correct.

Next.

Melodie! Yay! She said I can write about her. The song is "Lucky" by Njomza. I feel really lucky. I love you, Mel. She is a cool chick. She's been arrested too many times for some fucking bullshit, though. For real.

Actually I think I have loved a lot. Mel and I share a gay ex-boyfriend. It's complicated. Chaz. Chaz was sweet. I got mad when I was fucked up and destroyed his popsicle stick house when we lived together. Greer didn't really like him because he didn't do dishes. I'm sure many people have hated me for the same fucking reason, so whatever. Doing dishes sucks. Although I do Nicole's a lot.

I feel like Animal is the only one who might try to sue me because he said he didn't want me to include him. But, fuck. He's in a lot of my stories. I just haven't written about them yet. I did attempt to make a documentary while it was happening, though.

Anyway, I forgot what I was saying. Mel. I love Mel. Next.

I should write about Aglago. Oh my god. I just realized that. I could send a copy there. That would be so cool. I still remember the address. Whoever's music is playing right now I do not like at all. I should be more selective. Now I can only hear the rain. Gross, I think I ate a bugger.

So that's what I'm going to do. I'm going to write about whatever and then send copies of the book to the people I wrote about. I'll sign them so they'll be valuable once I'm dead. Booger. Not bugger. Whatever.

I miss all my old IRC friends. Those were the days. Afternet. #thecow, #rainbowroom, #fluke, #deadferretsaloon. Goddamn I miss those days so fucking much. 1997. That was a good year. That was a really good year. Alix. Jody. Liza. Cynthia Blair. That name sticks out. Oh, and this Greek girl Kathy. Or maybe it's a C. Sorry, I sent Alix a message asking or telling her that she's in my book, so I started thinking about Ottawa. Several of my IRC friends were there.

It's getting hot in here, so I'm going to take off some of my clothes–well, my jacket, anyway. I need music. And water. And maybe a cigarette, even though my chest hurts. My whole body hurts. I want to take another hot shower.

I miss Purim. That was a good day.

I took a hot shower and smoked a cigarette while doing so, as I do. I thought a lot about various subjects, as I do. And now I don't know what I should do, as I do.

I messaged my friend Daniel Gates to see if he wanted to be my literary agent. He might be Jewish. He says he is, but he was adopted. We met in rehab in Valdosta. I met a lot of really cool people there–especially the staff. The staff were awesome. At the time I was going to write a TV show based on life in a rehab. I've thought about doing the same for a psych ward, too.

My mind just went to thinking about Adelaide's connection with Bill Gates, but it is a very stressful topic that triggers me severly. My ears are burning. Don't they say that means that someone is thinking about you or something? Or talking, maybe. I bet people are talking about me.

If I could grow my own world, how would I make it? Who would populate it? Who are the Fillorians? I need some magician friends. I just realized how often I'll skip over a thought because of how nervous I am about talking about it–or usually a person. Sometimes an event. Lane said he'd read this book. Lane. I miss Lane.

Anyway, Daniel and I ended up living with this guy who spent all of his money on crack, so that didn't work out. Now he's basically homeless and bored in Dothan. That has to suck. He needs a job. I feel like I need to go to Georgia to write–maybe Florida. That'd be cool. I could see Alex. But Covid. And Philip. He's sick. They used to own the only gay bar in Middle Georgia. Randall was a bartender there (the one who was murdered). I had so many absolutely amazing nights there. I just sent a message to Alex telling him that I mentioned them. I think Philip and I are okay now. I'm not sure if there are two or one. Ls, I mean. Getting old sucks. It really, really does. Oh, supposedly there are tunnels connecting Rosa Hill cemetery to the old monastery or whatever and then to downtown. There was an entrance underneath the club. I never saw it, though. Spooky.

Now here come the thoughts about the Masons. That's another very stressful topic. I can't even even. All of the sudden I got really fucking anxious about telling the world about it. I don't know if it's a good idea. I just won't talk about my family. Or should I? Is family off-limits? It's too fucking stressful. I'm sorry. I can't handle it. Fuck. Should I show anyone this now or wait until I'm done? Who would read it? I do not know.

I need drugs. I need hard drugs. I want to go back to Georgia. I mean, I just want a pain pill. That's what I really want. Suboxone tastes like ass. Actually it's way worse than ass. Ass doesn't have to taste bad. I need music. Art. I miss Art's music.

I just told him I'd mention him in it. I was really high over at his house one night, and for some reason the scenario was that he and I might have to spend eternity together, and I freaked out. I was being super crazy. His gigantic step-mother came running out the house and grabbed me and made me leave. I left my shoes there.

Earlier that day I had posted on Facebook that I wanted to know what it was like to walk a mile in a black man's shoes. I went over to see my friend at the Royal Inn (she used to be a Playboy model, she says), and her black boyfriend let me borrow his shoes. They're still at my parents' house. I also owe them $10. I went to a psych ward before I could pay it back.

Now I'm listening to Bernia Blount's playlist. It's a cover of "Come Together" by Gary Clark Jr. Not bad. I don't really remember much about her. We went to high school together. I remember her being nice. We didn't talk much, I don't think. I like this song, even though it has bukkake undertones. Am I using people's full names based on how well I know them? I think I am. Why am I doing that? I need to black out my parents' names, for sure.

This song said something about flying like an eagle. It reminded me of Lori #2. I need to apologize to her. I was kind of a dick to her the other day, I think. A lot of shit was going down back in Georgia, and I was projecting, I think. She'd probably hate this book, but I think she's the incarnation of Mother Nature. That isn't kaballistically far off. But God is One. Or he will be called One, rather. That's what is supposed to happen. There is a mathematical equation I think may exemplify this, actually. It's Euler's theorem. Did I mention how you can derive pi, Euler's number, and alpha from Genesis 1:1 and John 1:1 of the Bible (the Hebrew and Greek numerical values, respectively). Yes, you can.

Alabama Shakes is playing on Bernie Blount's playlist. I like this music. "I Found You". Aww, I found you, Bernia Blount. Not Bernie. I mean, unless you want to be a man, although I think you look great as a woman. If you ever read this, you'll probably think I'm really weird.

I wonder what happened to Piss. I need to stop smoking so many goddamn cigarettes. I should probably talk about famous people more so publishers will like me. I really want some feedback to have motivation to keep going. I truly am severely afraid of writing about certain things, though. I don't know why. I mean, I definitely do know why. But still. Yeah. Fuck. No, I do not kiss my mother with a mouth like this. Bernia Blount sounds like a very wholesome person.

Bernia's playlist just told me to find a girl and settle down. Damn it, why can't I be straight? It fucking sucks. Steady as she goes. The Reconteurs. This sounds good, although maybe a little staged metaphysically or something. Am I tossing some word salad up in here?

I was just thinking about my dear friend Karla who worked at The Base. She is amazing. I would love to have her read this, but she is really wholesome, also. I feel bad. I feel like this novel is definitely not for wholesome people. That's it. Not for wholesome people.

I announced it to Facebook. Was that stupid? Should I remove it? Mel loved it. That's cool. God, I need to get someone to help me contact all these people and tell them I'm writing about them. Maybe I should stop talking about people so much. Not Mel. Mel is a good friend. Karla is too, but I think of her more as like a mom or something. A mom-friend. Is that weird? I'm just a little ashamed of some of the things I've said.

Next.

Damnit, I want to go back to Georgia. I also want to make paper copies so I can give one to Art. Art. Art is Art. I like art. I should go to galleries more often. Maybe Art and I can do that as long as it's wheelchair accessible.

Alex, the proprietor of Reaction/Synergy, the only gay club in Middle Georgia, said he wishes someone would write a book on 2000 to 2010– that ten year span. The drag queens would be the best people to ask. And of course Philip and Alex. It would involve a lot of sex and drugs and music. I can definitely tell you that for sure. For sure. I couldn't do it justice. It was this long dream of ecstasy and self-doubt. But lots of dancing. Hot bodies. Drag Queens. The drag queens are delicious. And hilarious. Deanna, of course, even though she's mad at me. Well, her boy-self is. Maybe he's not. I don't know. I don't know.

I don't like it when people are mad at me. I need to move my energy. Should I take the bus or fly? Oh, shit, no, I'm supposed to help them with stuff on March 6. I have to pick up the dog from the vet in Louisville. It's the little one that doesn't really like me. He's scared of me, although I gave him some fries earlier. Is there anyone besides my parents and Animal who don't want me to write about them? Well, I don't know if my dad would care. He's all about protecting the constitution. That should've been capitalized. Oh well. Words are fun. Synchronicity is fun. I just had a horrible idea about killing myself. Kids, don't kill yourselves.

Yay, Daniel says he'll be my literary agent. He isn't concerned about his security.

CHAPTER VI

I came over to the general store to have a sandwich and write. I'm a little nervous, mostly because my fingernail is still painted pink from where Adelaide was testing her polish. The people here seem to be very conservative. I am actually very nervous. One of the men is putting together a puzzle. His wife, I think, is using a calculator for something. Their son is making my sandwich.

I called Ellen earlier to ask her if it was ok for me to use her name. She said yes, as long as I didn't include her last name. I didn't. Nora messaged me, too. She's excited about it. I should write more about her. Timmy (Thomas's brother) called me from jail. His court case is next week. I need to put some money on his books. Wow, I feel really awkward here.

I shouldn't have come. I don't really need this sandwich, although I'm a little hungry. I should've just gone to Carefree to buy some cigarettes and get Subway or something. I don't like being the center of attention, really, even though I am writing a book about myself. I'm full of contradictions, though. Maybe it has something to do with being born on a cusp. Someone please get me out of here. Now I have to wait on my damn sandwich.

I think they're talking about their health inspection or something. I'm not really following their conversation. This is a really cute store, though. I like it. They have all kinds of stuff. Maybe I should've faced away from them when I sat down at the table. This is unbelievably awkward. I don't know why.

Nora told me to save my money for a publisher because they aren't cheap. Honestly, I have no idea how the business works. I just want to write my book and have people read it and not hate me. That's all. It's been pretty therapeutic so far. My sandwich is here.

I really don't feel like eating, but I have to be polite. Maybe I can down half of it. That's what I told the guy. I need help. My brain is so fucked up. I don't know how to be a good human. Moses thinks I have too much anxiety. He's probably right. Maybe I should tell my psychiatrist. I haven't spoken to her in a while. I wonder if I can write this whole novel in a week? Is it considered a novel? What is the difference between a novel and a book? Is it the length that matters? So many questions.

Fuck it, I might have one more bite, but then I'm out of here. I need a cigarette. I need to text Adelaide to make sure it's ok for me to take the truck. The Mercedes smells too much like gas. I can't deal, really. It's that bad. Yeah, I'll eat this later.

Okay, I'm home. I decided to get a pack of Adelaide's dad's Montclairs. Whatever. I'll buy him another one. He has several, and he told me the other day I could have a pack if I needed one. I feel like I'm wearing out my welcome. I accidentally left the gates open, and the dogs got out. Plus I apparently did something wrong when I tried to drive the Mercedes, and now it won't open.

I feel bad for Ellen. She was saying how Tom (her husband) just got out of the nursing home. He was in the hospital for a while. He has Parkinson's, I think. She was taking care of him when we spoke on the phone. I wonder what Ellen would think of my book, or if she would read it? I feel like it would seem too childish for her. She's very intelligent. I used to drive her Mini Cooper to Wegmans. Well, sometimes I went to Weis, but she definitely prefers Wegmans. I was briefly their house chef or something. Then I was the basement-dwelling IT vampire. I wonder if she is still smoking e-cigarettes. Vuse.

I was thinking last night how Frank Sinatra's "My Way" will probably be played at my funeral, unironically. I do identify with its lyrics, although I never really paid complete attention to them until last night–something about speaking your mind unlike those that kneel. I've definitely kneeled for God many times, just never in public or anything. I need some music.

I think I'm going to listen to Kate's playlist. That's Ellen's daughter. It's really good. "Cold Cold Water" by Mirah. Such a good song. Is it unbecoming that I don't always write in full sentences? I left the only home I knew. I stayed alive, now I found you. I wish someone would sing a song like that about me. Or maybe not. I don't know. You never know. I wonder if Kate will read my book. Maybe I could get some people I write about to read it and comment. I could put their quotes on the back of the book or something. That'd be neat.

I'm feeling a little dysphoric. Next song, although this is a really good song. Maybe I'll finish it. It is definitely tough to be in love. I was just reminded of a time when Kate and I stayed up all night talking about the transit of Venus in 2004. I thought there was some kind of hidden pattern, and I was going to discover it. Fucking Adderall.

Dresden Dolls is playing. "Good Day". I've seen them so many times in concert, but I discovered them through Kate. Greer loves them, too. I have a good memory of Greer, Kate, and I hanging out in Kate's room for three days even though we thought it was just one. Greer and I flew up to Boston with Franco to see them once. That was an amazing show–at the Bow & Arrow theater in Harvard Square. It was very theatrical and fancy. I definitely need something for my anxiety.

I just decided to put chapters in. The scroll idea seems kind of lame. Oh my fucking God. I love this song so much: "Wait at Milano" by Tim Barry. I was having a really bad night, and this came on. Thank you, Kate. I won't mention the time you yelled at me and I was going to freeze to death in the snow because I was suicidal. The psych ward I went to was really nice, though. Pennsylvania psychiatric hospitals are pretty good.

I want to be held by a guy. I want to feel loved in most ways. When you live this world alone, what will you take? Go out west, come May. Maybe I should. I haven't been out west in a while. It's been a couple years, I think. Wow, there are a lot of memories attached to that. But I still have several chapters left. Should I ask Sharon's sister to edit this? She's an editor. Sharon is the one whose son accidentally shot her. I could always redact the names. I wonder how much she would charge me. I feel like she might judge me, though, even though she's cool, and I got to see RENT for the first time with her and Sharon's daughter in NYC.

Elliot Smith is playing. "Between the Bars". I used that title in one of my songs. I wonder if he really killed himself. I've definitely felt like stabbing myself before. People that you've been before that you don't want around anymore, they push and shove and won't bend to your will. I concur. I need a drink. I need a goddamn corkscrew. Maybe I'll take my second shower of the day. I'm ready for Adelaide to get home from work.

Ellen says she doesn't read memoirs. I asked her how many words she thought should be in this. She does read a lot, and she said she's read several historical biographies. I have a feeling she'd think my book was trash. Maybe it is. I think it is. But it's my trash. My mind is trash. My soul is trash. I am trash. I'm white trash. Am I white trash? I asked Adelaide this yesterday. She said I shouldn't worry about what other people think. I think I am. I wish I didn't have to leave my bed or take my clothes off to take a shower. I am feeling very uncomfortable right now.

I'm going to take a shower. Fuck it. Their water bill is going to be high. Or maybe they have a well.

Okay, I feel better. I started listening to a gay music playlist on Spotify. There was some lesbian country song on, I guess. Now it's a song by Rae Spoon, "When I Said There Was an End to Love". It's pretty chill. I was daydreaming about getting a ticket back to Georgia. We're done watching The Magicians. I need more attention. I can hang out with Nicole if I go to Georgia. And I can hang out with other people, too. Maybe it'll trigger something for my book.

If I leave Sunday it'll be $111 from Corydon to Macon. That'll give me time to go pick up the dog from the vet in Louisville for Adelaide. I'm going to call my mom and see what she thinks. At first she didn't want me to come back home, but I think she's over it by now. That's another story.

She says everything's not going to be a party every day. She wants us all to get along. She said we did wonderful for almost a whole year until I stopped taking my medicine. She wants me to get my degree so I can see about myself and have a life. She wants me to send a picture of my Freewrite. I sent her one. I don't really know if she wants me to come back or not. She said other things, but I wasn't paying attention too much because I was typing what she was saying.

Oh, she also said she didn't want me to say anything too bad about me or my family. I feel like the worst thing I've said about myself is how much I like Opey's dick. That's pretty risque. And it's kind of gross to a lot of people, I'm sure. I get it. I do. I'm definitely not going to let my mom read my book. I feel kind of gross now. But I just got out of the shower.

My mom said I should write about my adventures, but I've mostly been writing about the fucked up shit that goes on in my head. I don't know which is more interesting, although my adventures have definitely been pretty interesting. I wish I could just live in the shower. Maybe I need a hot tub. Greer, Nicole, and I were supposed to go stay in this cabin in the mountains that had one, but Greer had to stay home to take care of her mom who has cancer, so we didn't go. Plus I kind of went crazy and got in a fight with my parents, so I had to leave town anyway. That's why I'm here.

I think I'm going to take this last little piece of a Suboxone I have. I just feel gross. It tastes so bad, though. I can't stand it. I started to read some of what I had written in part one, and I realized how choppy some of it sounds. I can't help it though–that's just how my mind works. My mind is choppy. Whatever. I used to write really well when I was younger. I won a RESA writing contest in eighth grade and an essay contest in literary in high school. I also got paid like $15 once for two articles: one about Los Angeles's public transportation and one about the time I met Chris Crocker. He was nice, although he seemed sad. He was also in NYC when I was there years ago. I met someone who was going to his party or something, but I didn't go.

It's dissolving in my mouth. Nevermind. I was going to puke, so I had to swallow it. I was told that it wouldn't work if I swallow it. It has to dissolve in your mouth, but it tastes so fucking bad. I hate it. Burnt meth is the only thing worse. I think I've mentioned that before. I need a cigarette and music.

I really want more feedback on what I'm writing. I think Art would have great feedback, but he can't get it to open on his phone. I was going to give him my Kindle to use when I go back to Georgia, but I don't know when that'll happen. Maybe Lane will want to read the first part, at least. I need to trim my toenails, but I don't know where the clippers are. My dad bought me a manicure set for Christmas, but I have misplaced it.

I had a pedicure once at the Four Seasons in Florida with my rich Jewish friend. It hurt. Lane lived with us at The Farm with her. Those were some crazy times. It was fun, though. We partied all the time, built fires, drank, sang, danced, and had plenty of sex. Supposedly the old tobacco barn was haunted. Kelsey tried to have a seance, but it didn't work, although the next day the barn door was open, and there were animal guts in the threshold. Kelsey goes by a different name now, and she probably still hates me for calling her a racial slur when I was really mad at her. I miss her, though. I miss The Farm.

I feel like hanging out with someone. I have separation anxiety, I think. I don't know. I'm just all sorts of fucked up. Maybe I should call my therapist and schedule an appointment. I'm doing that now.

The receptionist said she's going to send my therapist an email. This therapist is pretty nice. She is one of many, but I like talking to her sometimes. She is a very Southern Baptist. But she smokes cigarettes. I have no idea which religion is right, although I'm mostly drawn to Judaism these days. I'd love to talk to Jesus, though. I miss Adelaide.

I wonder if this Suboxone is going to do anything since I swallowed it. I guess I could always eat another gummy, but it's pretty early in the day for that. I feel weird being high around Adelaide's dad sometimes, but he knows I got them when we went to Michigan. He just doesn't want me to drive his truck with anything illegal on me. Adelaide says it's food, so it doesn't count.

I need to wash these sheets. I haven't washed them since I moved in. Timmy used to sleep in this bed, so most of the funk is probably his and the dogs. Timmy is cute, but he's very straight and young. Good for Adelaide. She says his dick is really nice, although he won't let her take a picture. She always shows me dick pictures. That's one of the reasons I love her. I'm such a fucking pervert. Gross. I want to go to Jewish Hell. I want my soul to be cleansed.

I should call Ronda to see if she is okay with me mentioning her in my book. She was my rehab mom in Palm Desert. I don't know why I just thought of her. I'll text her instead. Maybe I should go back to Rehab in Valdosta. I'd go to the one in Moultrie, but it's not co-ed except for the psych ward. I had a good time there. I met some cool people like Bethany, although it was a bit scandalous when I went over to the guy's side because I fell in love with this supposedly heterosexual Buddhist guy.

He was a writer. He wrote a poem about me, and our arms touched while we were watching some AA video. But then he started telling people how I had a crush on him, and it really embarrassed me. He was kind of a dick. I don't even remember his name. I want to take another shower. My body just really hurts. It sucks. I wish I knew another way to produce endorphins other than masturbating. I'm too lazy to run. I'm going to call Amy.

I almost called my sister because they have the same name. But I'm not going to write about my family, per my mom's wishes. I love my sister.

Amy is Lori and Naomi's mom, by the way. Naomi kissed Clementine, and Lori lives in Bristol. She put me on hold. She said I can use her name, but she asked whose picture I'm going to put on the book since I'm using a pseudonym. I told her I might take a picture of myself where you can't see my face. Damn, I've been on hold for a long ass time. What is she doing? I just sneezed. I smoke too much. Maybe she's peeing or something. Did I already mention Clementine? Amy knows her. She's Cybil Shepherd's daughter. I don't think I have to ask them for permission to use their names since they're famous, although I told Clementine I was going to mention her. She doesn't talk to me. Watch her try to sue me or something. My dad says you can't squeeze blood out of a turnip, but what if I actually make money for this? Could they take away my disability? I don't think so. Clementine, if you read this, please don't sue me. I think you are cool. I just wish you would talk to me sometime. I know you think I'm a drama queen. But so are you. You are a literal drama queen. You're an actress. Well, you were an actress. Your job was to be a drama queen. Why am I still on hold?

I love you, Amy, but I'm about to hang up the phone. This is getting ridiculous. How long have I been on hold? I have no concept of time.

I remember I met Clementine at this New Years Eve party in Atlanta. She had brought some Absinthe back from Europe. DJ Dangermouse was spinning. I got a copy of his Grey Album, but I lost it. Actually I think I lost two copies. That sucks, because I think it's worth a lot of money now since it's banned or whatever. I think it's banned. Jay-Z tried to see or some shit. I don't remember. Ok, I'm hanging up. She can call back.

Awesome. Ronda says I can mention her in my book, as long as it's good (just kidding). I love Ronda. She is awesome. She's been sober for a long time, and she's a MILF. If I were straight I'd totally mack on her. On New Years Eve when I was in rehab, we played beer pong with energy drinks. I thought I was going to have a heart attack. Red Line is the devil. That shit is so strong. It's very methy. I'm surprised it's legal. Ronda always drank Bang drinks, though. She was addicted to those and these fancy sparkling waters in cans. Blood orange was my favorite. She would let me have one sometimes.

My dead boyfriend's sister Jen just messaged me on Facebook asking how I've been doing. She used to hate me, but now she's okay with me. I know she misses Josh. They all do. I should probably change their names since I mentioned his dad giving him pills. I really like his family, and I don't want them to dislike me. Josh had a lot of pain. It's not like his dad is a bad dad or anything. My mom used to give me pain pills, too. In fact, she would hide them in pieces of tinfoil around the house for me to find while she and my dad were on vacation. It was like an Easter Egg hunt. Josh was my boyfriend who died, in case you've forgotten. I know I talk about a lot of people. There have just been a lot of people in my life. Fuck it, I'm going to take another shower.

That was nice. I feel a little better. I also messaged Cheri's sister to see if she would edit my book–or to see how much she would charge, at least. She's pretty cool. She also saves birds for a living. That is definitely respectable. Twice I have attempted to deliver injured birds to her, but they never made it. She is also a proud Southerner with a very awesome Southern name. It sounds like Wanda but better. Ew, a stink bug or something just crawled across my keyboard. I feel a lot better, though. I'm probably going to be reincarnated as a bee, although I'd rather be a barren woman, I think. My Jewish therapist in Bethlehem says God loves me. I don't know if that is true. I just don't know.

I always think of people I want to write about that probably wouldn't want me to mention them, like my old math teacher who is a Jehovah Witness. I don't think it's okay to write that name if you're Jewish, but they say no one really knows how to pronounce the true name. It probably sounds something like ee-yah-who-way, but I could be wrong. That's just a guess. Hashem is his name. Hashem means "The Name" in Hebrew. I'm hungry, but I don't feel like eating. I need some fingernail polish remover. My mind is dumb.

I wish something really cool would happen so I could have a plot. I mean, I know memoirs don't really need to have plots–at least not at the present moment–but I think a plot would be cool, as long as it's not negative in any way. Although people do like to read about fucked up shit. I wonder if my language is too crass for Wanda. She reminds me of a Southern Belle but more of a tomboy. I just hope she doesn't charge too much to edit. I'm pretty poor–well, relative to others in my country, at least. I'm ready for my stimulus check, although it will probably all go towards fixing my teeth.

Maybe I should go ahead and take a picture of myself for my book. I don't know how to do that, though. I should probably wait and get Adelaide to do it or something. Is putting a picture of myself on my book stupid? I mean, I won't show my face, although I do have a really cute picture of my face that would be great. I just don't want my family to get upset that I'm writing this. It can be pretty perverse.

I hope I'll have fans–just not crazy fans that will want to hurt me. I want to be loved. I just got an email from the Publishers Clearing House. I never check them, because I'm not a very lucky person. I spent $20 on a slot machine at the Las Vegas airport and lost it in like thirty seconds. I spent $60 at a casino on the Mississippi River with my dad. I actually snuck back down to play when he was going to bed. I lost it all, although at one point

I was up to about $100 or something. It was the Wonder Woman game. That was fun.

I have 23 new messages. That is one of my favorite numbers. The other one is 42, for obvious reasons. So cliche. Thank you, Douglas Adams. He wrote some of the only books I've ever actually finished. I'm clearly entirely too ADD to read a book, much less write one, although that's what I'm doing, kind of. Is it ADD or ADHD? I never really understood the distinction. Am I hyperactive? It depends on my mood, I guess, as do most things. Do I annoy people? How many people will read this? I have absolutely no idea. It'd be funny if they used it in school one day. It'd have to be college, though, for sure, even though I feel like I write like a twelve year old or something. I'm going to Google how to self-publish, I think. Paul always told me I should be a producer. Paul is Moby's friend. I just sent him an email to tell him I wrote about him. I think he's told me before that I could.

Once I told him he could make a movie about me without telling me. For a while I thought that he and David Lynch had secretly teamed up to do that. There were people following me around with cameras, but it's because I got high and signed a release form without reading it. I should probably tell that story. This is going to be a long chapter.

So when I was homeless in 2011 in Venice Beach, this non-profit gave some of us shittie digital video cameras to document our experience. A couple years later, when I moved back to LA with the guy I was dating (he was an actor), I remembered I had the footage, so I took it to the non-profit. They were excited and told me to come back in a week.

I go back, and there is this camera crew there. It was this famous Palestinian actress called Hiam Abass and Jean Baptiste, this director. They filmed me while asking me questions, and they had me read some poem by some famous author. Then I played "Non, Je Ne Regrette Rien" by Edith Piaf on my ukulele, which I always took with me everywhere I went. Jean Baptiste was pacing back and forth on the phone, but I think they liked it.

They ended up showing me on the screen at some production they did at the Masonic Lodge at Hollywood Forever Cemetery. I didn't go, but my friend went, and he said they were giving out drinks and everything. I guess it was pretty fancy.

Anyway, one day I got in a fight with my boyfriend, the actor. He was on The Walking Dead. I went down to the boardwalk and was sitting at Jan's bench (Jan was my street mom and the first female punk rock DJ in the world). Jan was dead, though, and I was sitting in her spot crying. Then all of the sudden, Hiam comes and sits by me and tries to console me. I thought it was really nice, until I looked up and saw a camera in my face. It really upset me, and I stormed off. For a while I thought people were following me around with cameras. Maybe they were. I don't know.

There's actually a lot about that time I could write about. I could write about how my boyfriend got shitfaced on a bottle of Vodka from CVS and beat the shit out of me in Santa Monica. We had been staying in this artist guy's truck, but he was asleep in the back. I had two broken ribs. I called my mom, and she got me a red eye flight back to Atlanta. He ended up getting arrested a while later for assault and battery or something. It was someone else, though. I don't really feel like writing about this anymore.

Happy thoughts. Happy thoughts. Happy thoughts. Kittens. Cotton candy. I haven't been to a fair in a while. I like rides. The Gravitron is okay, although it makes me feel a little weird. I wonder when they're going to have a fair again, since, you know, Covid. By the way, about as many people here wear masks as they do back in my hometown in Georgia. It's whatever, I guess. So many opinions. Fuck, I hate The Walking Dead. I've never even watched it. He said if I ever tried to contact him again, he'd destroy me. That was after I offered to buy him a ticket to come back to Georgia. Allegedly he ended up getting stabbed while he was homeless out there. I really did love him, I think. Oh, and he gave me syphilis.

Now my mind is flooded with all kinds of memories I don't really want to have or talk about, even though I know I probably should. That's what makes interesting reading, right?Fuck. I need a hug. And I want to cry, but I can't cry on command. Greer can. I'd call her, but she doesn't have service, and I doubt she'd answer anyway. She's like that. Maybe I should go back to Georgia, although it doesn't seem like my mom really wants me to come back yet. I don't know. I don't know what I should do. I don't know who to ask.

I don't know how to pronounce Phrenocosmia, really, even though that's going to be the title of my book. I should probably tell you why I chose that name. I'm going to smoke a cigarette first, though. I'm also really hungry, but as I've said, I don't feel like eating.

I just spoke to Michelle on the phone. She was at the rehab I went to in Palm Desert. She remembered how they had to come pick me up from Venice Beach when I ran away to be homeless (again). I had forgotten about that. Michelle is cool. She took Andrew and me out to Olive Garden once. She's divorcing her husband and with a guy who seems to be making her happy. Her husband told her he wasn't in love with her anymore, which is ridiculous. Michelle is a very lovable woman.

Andrew. I was so in love with him, even though he was straight. I slept in the bunk above his, although at one point it got too intense sleeping in the room with a bunch of guys I was attracted to, so I moved out into a tent in the backyard by the pool. That was great. Ronda always brings it up. I miss that tent.

Oh, at the time I was dating this Mexican Gypsy who thought he was psychic. He also had dissociative identity disorder. One of his identities didn't like me very much. Anyway, he told me that my family had a generational curse that affected us financially. I got really upset when I heard this, so I frantically ran around the pool, and in my head I was cursing the cursers and trying to undo the curse at the same time.

An hour later, my mom called me and told me that the city had been working on the sewage system, and the pipes backed up and ruined our basement. They ended up getting a bunch of money for it, though, that they used to renovate the basement and put on a new roof. I always wondered if those two events were connected in some magical way.

Andrew, though. He was so beautiful, although he had been a pretty bad heroin junkie. He was my best friend for a while. Once he held my hand and squeezed it really tight. It hurt. I can't remember why he did that, but I was happy for him to hold my hand for a second. I hear he's doing well now, although I haven't talked to him in a long ass time.

I just played and sang a cover of "Where is my Mind" by The Pixies on my ukulele. I feel better. That song reminds me of the time (jailbird) Timmy, possibly Opey, and I went to the abandoned Central State Hospital in Milledgeville. We were going to make a music video of me singing there, but we didn't.

There was a famous serial killer that killed a bunch of people in my family that died there. I probably shouldn't mention her name, though. Well, I guess I can. Her name is Anjette Lyles. Is that too much? I just don't want my family reading this. I am ashamed. Anyway, we went to see a play about her once when my grandfather was alive. He didn't want to go, even though we had free tickets. I found out she was into Voodoo, apparently, which is pretty interesting. She poisoned my grandfather's aunt, her husband, and her daughter with arsenic, I think. That must've been a huge tragedy for my family. It was all for insurance money, too, allegedly. I just realized how many damn people and events I've yet to write about. Shit. I'm a mess. Currently listening to Rufus Wainwright's "Cigarettes and Chocolate Milk". I like him. I want some chocolate milk. I always want a cigarette.

I just remembered I never told you why I'll probably name

my book Phrenocosmia. First of all, I'm extremely addicted to genealogy. I've done countless friends' genealogies. Once I did Kim's, and I found this cousin she had that died in the 1930s. I had a vision about her, and I wrote a song about her. Her name was Maragaret Eleanor Lee, and she lived in California. She was in a club in college called the Phrenocosmian Society or something. It means "world of the mind" in Greek, I think. I just like the way it sounds. She was very beautiful. She kind of reminds me of Lilly. Lilly was best friends with Greer and I back in high school. She also kind of looks like Janis Joplin (Lilly, not Margaret). Although Lilly did like to channel Margeret Mitchell a lot for some reason. I miss her. She also used to drive with her feet and read the dictionary. I just informed her that she's in my book. She's probably at work. She replied, "Of course it is." to my hope that it's okay that I write about her. That's cool. I knew she'd be okay with it. Maybe I'll write more about her later.

CHAPTER VII

Adelaide finally came home, and we went to Dollar General, where I bought a corkscrew, finally. I'm drinking straight out of the bottle. It's a 2019 Louis Jadot Beaujolais from Walmart. Classy. I tried chugging it, but it's more of a sipper. It's a little bitter and watery, but I'm definitely not a wine connoisseur. Adelaide is making weird noises to the dogs downstairs. Some chill music is playing on my laptop. "Map on a Well" by Lucy Dacus. I think this is still the gay playlist.

When I would visit my rich Jewish friend's mother's house in Buckhead, I would sometimes drink Merlot and listen to French music by myself. One night, though, I was drinking and took the gay virginity of the heir to a very famous kosher foods company. He was cute.

She's not rich nor very Jewish anymore, though, since her dad died. She's doing well, though, I think. I hear she's sober. Her dad had a seat on the Chicago stock exchange and smoked crack. I'm not really sure what it means to have a seat on a stock exchange, but it sounds pretty important. She's awesome, though. She went to rehab when she was like thirteen or something. She's a trooper. I miss her. I guess this wine isn't that bad, as long as you sip it.

I'm feeling a little sad or something. I'm not entirely sure why. Maybe I need new music or something. I miss my guitar. I left it at the last guy I dated's house. We were pretty incompatible, but at least he has a guitar now. I have two shirts he gave me, his cologne, and a ridiculously expensive beach sand scooper for metal detecting he bought me for Christmas. We had planned on going to the beach, but the relationship only lasted like a month. I like metal detecting. Jesus has my old metal detector, but my parents bought me a new one for Christmas. Of course, I got to open it a couple weeks before Christmas because I'm spoiled like that.

My old math teacher, the Jehovah Witness, told me she was going to Paypal me some money for doing some genealogical research for her. I told her she didn't have to, but she insisted. I said I'd use the money to pay for an editor. She's really nice. I really like reading the daily message on the Jehovah Witness website. I'm not so sure about their concept of 144,000, though. In the Book of Revelation, it says they will be virgins, never having defiled themselves with women. The JWs think it's a metaphor for the Catholic Church or "Christendom", though. Who knows? I do like that they don't think Jesus was God. I don't think he thought he was God, either. But I guess I could be wrong. I would really like to hang out with Jesus. Both Jesuses, really. I have a lot of pain and questions. I want to take a shower, but I need to stop using so much water. I found out they don't have a well. I told Adelaide's dad I'd pay the water bill. He said it'd be $60 or $70, but I don't mind at all. I'm thankful they're letting me stay here rent-free.

I just want to be held. I really do. I want to feel loved, physically. Antony and the Johnsons is playing now. I really dig his or her voice. So pleasant. Will anyone ever hold me again? It would feel so damn nice. Once I met this guy from Facebook while I was crazy. We had sex, during which he focused on my shins way too much for some reason. But afterwards I spooned him and cried. It felt like Heaven, but he never really talked to me again. I called him from the psych ward a week or so later, but I think he only answered because he didn't recognize the number.

I want some heroin. I say "I" a lot. But this book is about me, so there. Adelaide's Timmy apparently likes to make jokes about how much I always want drugs. I hope he never experiences the kind of pain I experience. Maybe I should take another fucking shower. Oh, I masturbated before I started this chapter. I felt better for like fifteen minutes. Adelaide claims girls' orgasms are like twenty times stronger than guys. She says her afterglow sometimes lasts for days. I'm severely jealous. I wish I were a woman, damnit. I would love to be a woman. Too bad I'm losing my head hair.

I should get my Neurontin filled on Wednesday. I have to take at least three of them at a time for it to do anything, so I run out in a week or two every month. I would tell my psychiatrist about it, but I don't want her to cut me off. I had a referral for a pain clinic through my doctor once, but I ended up in the psych ward so I missed my appointment. Actually I don't think I ever got an appointment. I waited for months, though.

Fuck it. I'm going to take another shower. How many does that make today? It's only 8:20. I need a hot tub. Oh, my friend Scott is typing. I told him I mentioned him in my book. I wonder what he's going to say. I don't remember if I mentioned him by name or what I said about him. And I'm not entirely sure if he'd care about what I may have men tioned about him since it involved gay stuff, and he's not really gay. He's typing really slow. The shower is warming up. I was going to wait for his reply before I got in, but fuck it. Too slow.

I feel better. I took a shower. Scott said he didn't mind me mentioning him. He says what I'm doing is really cool, and he thinks everyone should do it actually. Also my friend Paul emailed me back. He wants his last name to be Fairchild and hopes that I write about him kindly. I have nothing unkind about Paul to say, although I wonder if he would mind if people knew that we did it once. I don't know if I should elaborate because that might be a bit too much. I sent him a copy of my first part to peruse. I really want to know if he has a kid. I'm pretty sure he doesn't. His email signature looks very professional, though. AFI Director/Writer. Fancy. I like his movies and him. He's a cool cat.

I'm really hungry. I think the only thing I've eaten today was a couple bites of a sandwich from next door. I should just drink my wine and be happy. I wish I could just chug it. I want a buzz. Ugh.

Holy. Fucking Shit. Crazy synchronicity. Once Paul told me my theme song was "Smalltown Boy". A cover of it by Orville Peck is playing on the gay playlist. That's crazy. Holy shit. That's so awesome. It's crazy how the universe works. I definitely identify with this song. For sure. It's my theme song. Yep. I have definitely cried to my own soul a lot. I wish I could cry on command. Damn you, Greer. Paul knows Greer. He says she reminds him of one of her best friends or something. Her Facebook bio says, "I'm a sarcastic, funny bitch that will disembowel you, so shut your face." I can't really see her disemboweling anyone, though, except for maybe a child molestor. She has an intense dislike for child molestors.

I wish I could just inject alcohol into my bloodstream. I haven't been drunk in a long time. A memory popped into my head of my birthday at The Farm. It was so cold outside, and I just lay down in the grass for a long time. People kept trying to bring me inside, but I wouldn't move because I felt so good. That was a good day. We usually drank Evan Williams, although one girl liked Ancient Age. The current song I'm listening to just mentioned whiskey. I love synchronicity, although sometimes it can be a little weird, I guess. "All-American Boy" by Steve Grand, in case you're wondering. Are all these people gay? He sounds like someone I wouldn't mind cuddling me. For sure. I Googled a picture of him. He has large arms, and he's thirty. Not a bad age. Yes, he can definitely cuddle me. Please and thank you.

I just sent him a message on Facebook. I'm going to have so many dates lined up once I'm famous. Ha. I doubt he'll even see it. You never know, though.

Lucy just texted me. She's been in my life for many, many years. We met at school back in 2005, I think. Oh, wait, I mentioned her in the last part. So one time we went on this school trip to

Atlanta for a conference. We went out and ended up at this sex club. We didn't know it was a sex club, and I think everyone thought she was my pimp because she was wearing this fur coat and hat, and I was a little twink.

We had to be at a meeting in a few hours, so we went to the headshop to get something to keep us up. They gave us something called Red Dawn Vector. We took them, and by the time we got back to the hotel, we were tripping balls. Everything looked like an Erector Set, and her face turned into a flower. That was insane. I love Lucy. She's the one with the Nazi grandpa or whatever, by the way. She's not a Nazi, though.

I'm watching Paul's director reel. It's pretty good. The song playing is okay. Lucy says she wants royalties if I get big. I would love to hand out royalties. I also want to have a giant party with everyone I've mentioned. That'd be a dream come true, literally. I actually wrote a song about that, which I think I mentioned in the first part. I kind of want to masturbate again. I love endorphins. Adelaide said I should try cuddling with the dog to produce oxytocin, but she needs to bathe him first. For sure.

Lucy wants me to make her a "superspy Bondbitch" and lie my ass off. Maybe that'll be Book Two. I wonder if Paul has read any of my book yet. I hope he likes it if he does. He always sent me his scripts to read, but I never read them because I suck and never read long things. I feel like talking to someone on the phone. I just don't know who would be available at the moment.

Larkin thinks the average novel length is 30,000 words, but he was drunk when he said that. I wish I were drinking with him right now. That'd be awesome. He's a brilliant alcoholic fag who has been there for me through thick and then. He's also a little Jewish. My therapist said I need to hang out with gay Jewish people. He's the only one I knew, although he's not an official Jew or anything. Daniel is kind of gay, but he's not an official Jew, either. Speaking of which, I think he's going to be a terrible literary agent. I haven't heard back from him. He's not really gay, but I did kind of have a crush on him when I met him in rehab.

I want to take another shower. I just really like showers. They make me feel better. I like the combination of water and fire. I also like air and earth, though. All the elements are pretty nifty and necessary, but for some reason fire and water are just so damn appealing. Fuck it, I'm going to do it. I'm insane. But I'm paying the water bill, so I don't feel so bad. I like having my own bathroom. It's pretty sweet.

I feel better. I kind of want to eat a gummy, but that might ruin the theme of this chapter. I don't know. I should just chug this wine, even though it's gross. My friend Michael just sent me a message about the tents that some high school bands are using because of Covid. Michael is a genius. We've had pretty good conversations at the Huddle House before. He thinks the universe is deterministic. He says it's fine that I've mentioned him. That reminds me of my other friend Michael that I went to rehab with last year, I think. I should call him. I wonder if it's too late.

Yay, he answered. And his odometer hit 250,000 miles while we were talking. I love him so much. He gives the best hugs, too, even though he's super skinny. But he's married. Alas. He is so dreamy. But he's a good friend. I really like talking to him. I developed an enormous crush on him when we were locked up together. I just liked being near him. I told him my deepest, darkest thoughts, and he's still my friend. That says something. This was during the time I thought I was the reincarnation of King David. Josh, my dead boyfriend, had also gone to the same hospital. If Michael weren't straight and married, I would give my left nut for him to be in my bed right now and cuddle me. He wants to get drunk whenever we hang out. You never know, I guess. Let a boy dream.

Wanda messaged me back. She wants me to send a few pages so she'll know what kind of editing to recommend. The price depends on the word count. I told her it was kind of risque and has a little sex talk. She's definitely the one I'd want to edit, though, as long as she's okay with it. I just hope she doesn't get upset that I mentioned Cheri and Allen. I just sent her Part One. I'm nervous. God it was so good to talk to Michael, though. I kind of want to close my eyes and touch myself and think about hugging him for a bit. Gross. I'm gross. Sorry, Michael. I really don't mean to objectify you. I guess I'm just a little tipsy.

Okay, I may have masturbated a little, but I didn't cum. I was mostly thinking about lying in bed with him with my arm across his chest as his wife sat there watching. Then I thought a little about his wife riding him while I made out with him. He sent me a picture of his new tongue ring a while back, so I thought of that, too. The heart wants what the heart wants. Desperate desire (that was a lyric to the song I'm listening to, by the way). "Love is a Fire" by Brandy Clark. Love is definitely a fire. Oh, Michael said he likes earth signs. His wife is a Taurus, too, although I'm right on the cusp. Why am I always into straight guys? It's tragic, really.

It's okay. We can just be friends. I need to find some new music. The playlist I'm listening to started over. I don't know what I want to hear, though. I really liked this playlist. I should listen to gay things more often. Maybe I can try to find another gay playlist. Alright, I found a GAY SHIT playlist. I don't know if I like it, though. I wonder if Adelaide's still awake. It's almost 11. I should drink more wine.

I want to go back to Georgia and hang out with Michael. I hope he won't be too weirded out when he reads everything I just wrote. I can't help it. That's just how my brain works. I'd settle for a hug. I've only drank half of this bottle. I'm such a lightweight pussy. Pussy sounds like such a misogynistic word. Pussy. Cunt. Cunt is probably one of the most powerful words. I very rarely use it. I just asked Michael to send me a new picture of himself. Is that weird? The other ones he sent me are on my old phone, which I gave to Nicole's kid after I reset it, of course. Maybe I should cum. Or take a shower. I need endorphins. I'm an endorphin junkie.

Nevermind. I think I'm too drunk or something. I came close, but not quite. I really hope Michael doesn't think I'm objectifying him by fantasizing about him. He's just who's on my mind at the moment. I have a hard time controlling my mind–not that I've been trying. It's whatever. I love you, Michael, even if you weren't adorable.

I keep glancing at my pink pinkie nail. It's pretty. I'm bored. I don't know why. I want to be hanging out with people. I miss parties. Parties are fun. I used to get so slutty at them, though, obviously. I should've been a Scorpio. Michael's a Scorpio. I'd get on Grindr, but Grindr is kind of gross and disappointing. So there's that. Fuck it, I will anyway. My old drug dealer is on there, but I think he blocked me. He freaked out on me, I guess out of guilt that we did it. He is mostly straight and just got out of prison. He likes transgendered people, though.

Hey, there's a cute guy who's three miles from me. It says he's new. Adelaide's dad said I'm not allowed to have gay sex in the house, though. I don't really want to have sex with a stranger anyway. I don't really want to have sex that much at all. I just want to cuddle with someone I love and am attracted to. I want that really fucking bad. You don't even know. Or maybe you do. I'm sorry if you do. Maybe I'll call my ex. Nah, I've been calling him too much lately–Moses, I mean. I'll call Franco.

I almost accidentally dialed the LDS Elders. I was interested in them for a while. They're really cute, but I'm not sure if Joseph Smith was a con artist or not. They all seem super sweet and like they genuinely believe in it, though. Okay, I'm calling Franco.

It went to voicemail. Maybe I should take yet another shower. Oxytocin is what I really need. I want to be loved. I can't state that enough. So pathetic. But I'm human. We're social creatures. It's in our DNA possibly. Ugh. Fine, I'm taking a shower. Fuck. I waste so much water.

I feel better. I think I might buy a ticket back to Georgia tomorrow. YOLO. Yes, I want a hug from Michael, but I also want to hang out with some other friends and be in a different environment so I can finish this book. Should I call my mom now or ask Adelaide first and make sure she's okay with it? I think she'll be okay. Maybe she can find someone else to pick up the dog from the vet. But yeah, I can see when Michael is off again. I'm insane. All for a hug. No, I like his conversation, too. Plus I wouldn't mind meeting his wife. He just sent me a picture of them. They're a cute couple. I'm not going to try to be a homewrecker. Definitely not. Besides, I'm almost certain he's completely straight.

I'm tired. Maybe I'll cut this chapter short and watch some Golden Girls or something. I can also drink the other half of my bottle tomorrow.

CHAPTER VIII

I can't sleep. I'm not drunk anymore, and I can't stop thinking about how disgusting I am for what I said in the last chapter. Seriously. I'm trying to take my mind off of it by watching the Golden Girls, but my mind won't shut up. Sex is stupid. I wish I were innocent and pure. I wish I didn't have lustful thoughts. My entire being just really hurts. Thoughts about being in a womb are coming up. I want to feel connected to someone and safe and warm without perversion. I wish someone would fix me. Does God even exist? I need a god. I need a savior. I hate myself. Why does the Golden Girls theme song sound like it's being sung by someone different? I hate this reality. I miss Randall. He loved this show. What can I do to make this feeling go away? Samson the dog just came upstairs. That made me feel a little better. I'm going to try to actually sleep now, maybe.

CHAPTER IX

I just woke up. It's 12:30 in the afternoon, and my face feels numb. I don't think I'll be finishing that bottle of wine. Maybe I'm making too much of a big deal out of it, but I just don't want to embarass myself anymore. I can write my memoirs without sexually fixating on straight friends. I've had a problem with that my entire adult life—well, longer than that, actually.

It's really cold in my room. It snowed here a couple weeks ago, but then it warmed up slightly. At least it's not as cold as the time I was in Chicago for New Years with my rich Jewish friend. I should really stop calling her that, but it was funny for a minute, I thought. Her boyfriend and I ended up talking to Russian prostitutes all night at the bar at The W hotel. There's more I could say about this subject, but I don't want any mafia to come after me or anything.

The episode where Blanche is trying to write a romantic novel is on. I feel like her. This seems like it's becoming a disaster. I would give up, but I've already written so much. Hormones suck. I guess that's what I should blame, anyway. The amount of "I" statements is starting to annoy me, even though this is about myself and all. Still, there should be a better variety of sentences, probably—like this one. Drivel. It's all drivel.

Blanche wants to go to NYC with Dorothy to write, since it's a writer's haven. That's actually not a bad idea. I'd go, but I'm not sure if I have any friends left there that actually like me, and I can't afford to stay at a hotel. AirBNB blocked my account because I tried to pay like $200/month for Zuckerberg's old house in San Jose. It's not my fault the ad was incorrect.

Whatever.

This is also the episode where Dorothy thinks she might be crazy. It's interesting how they viewed mental illness back then. It was definitely much more taboo than it is now, although it still could be better. Did I ever mention all the disorders I have? I probably did, but I'll do it again. Schizoaffective Disorder, ADHD, PTSD, and Borderline Personality disorder, probably. I've had a couple psychiatrists think I have BPD, but it takes a while to diagnose you, and I'm usually not in the same place for very long. I do have all the symptoms.

I've decided I'll just write for a week. That should give me enough words for this to be considered a book. Maybe my therapist will call me back. I think I need to switch my meds or something. My intrusive thoughts have been extremely annoying lately. My brain never shuts up. It does help that I can write some of them out, though. Meanwhile, I'm going to go take my first shower of the day. Oh, someone just messaged me as I was typing that. It's Andrew, the straight guy I was obsessed with in rehab in Palm Desert. He says, "of course" I can write about him. That's good. He even sent a little heart emoji. Okay, shower time.

Aw, Adelaide texted me from Corydon. She's about to go to the tanning bed, and she offered to bring me back some lunch. That's sweet of her. Oh, damn, I think I saw it too late. I never told her what I wanted. She said we can go back if I want, though. Oh, well.

It's so cold in this room. Both heaters are broken, I think. Well, I turned one of them on–the kind that looks like a fake fireplace–but it's making a weird noise. It's probably a fire hazard. I really need to clean up this room. It's trashy as hell, just like me. Pity party, I know. Shut up. I just have no energy right now whatsoever. I want to brush my teeth, but my toothbrush is downstairs, and I don't feel like getting out from under the covers. Woe is me. I wonder if Andrew will read my book, and if he'll get jealous when he realizes I obsess over other guys, too. I highly doubt it.

I wonder what Wanda will think. I'm not sure if she really pays attention to what the author is saying while she's editing, though. Maybe she doesn't. Hi, Wanda.

Adelaide wants to go to the music store. I'm reminded of Whit, the guy who gave me the North Star tattoo on my wrist. Well, he tried to do it with a needle and thread, but it sent electric jolts through my body, so I made him stop before he was finished. He's the reason I started playing the ukulele in the first place. But then he went to Brazil, and I fell apart because I'm such a pansy or something.

Whit wrote a couple songs about me–well, one, for sure. Half of it was basically a suicide note that I wrote to him, and the rest was his response. He wrote another Happy Birthday song with my name in it, but he claimed it was for his other lover with my name in NYC. I still don't know if he was joking or not, but I was pissed. I'm pretty much over it now, though. He's doing well, I guess, selling art in Chicago. He's from Louisville, though, and sometimes I secretly hope I'll run into him there. I really need to brush my teeth. Yay, Adelaide's home I think.

Okay, I ended up riding with her to Corydon where she bought this pretty red 3/4 size guitar from the music shop. The owner asked me where I was from, and when I told him, he asked if I took a wrong turn somewhere. I've taken several wrong turns. I played the last song I wrote for Adelaide while we were waiting on our to-go food from the Overlook. I snapped a picture for Facebook of the gorgeous view of the Ohio River. I realized one of the verses of my song is not entirely untrue, although I doubted its veracity for a bit.

I've been through the fires of Hell

I've got stories that I won't tell

I've broken ribs and broken hearts

I've been between the bars

But all that's left of me

Is this worn-out symphony

And a feeling that won't sway

Should I go, or should I stay?

I never know whether or not I should stay or go. I have a massive problem with that. Michael texted me back and told me he was off Thursday-Saturday or something. I don't know if I should go back to Georgia right now, though. Oh, and Wanda emailed me back with a quote for editing. I didn't realize it was that expensive. It's only a penny per word, but that adds up pretty fast. There's no way my mom would let me use my money for that probably, so I emailed another agency. We'll see what happens.

I have tremendous self-doubt. Clearly my writing style isn't nearly as advanced as the classics or anything, but I'm trying to be as real as possible, even if it is embarrassing as Hell. Oh, I also bought a pack of American Spirits because they didn't have any Chesterfields. I don't think they're poisoned, though. By the way, the reason I thought they were poisoned is because when I was out of my mind, the lady working at Flash Foods was telling me about how a representative from their company came by and told them how they wore masks while sprinkling the menthol over the tobacco while making the cigarettes. That just sounded really sketchy to me. I've also had numerous possible signs from God or the Universe that I should quit smoking.

Once a fox ate an entire pack that I left on the back porch. Then the next night he just looked at me and kept barking when I tried to smoke again. Another time I had been reading the Torah and came to a part about sending your seed through the fire. I thought that happened to me, and I thought it had something to do with smoking cigarettes. Then I went to Dollar General, and this guy came up to me and asked me if he could bum a cigarette.

He said his name was Moloch, the false idol to which Israelites would send their children through the fire, apparently. Fuck I just realized how disgusting my sheets are. I need to clean.

Adelaide gave me some kind of Stacker energy pill, so I don't have much of an appetite even though my stomach feels empty. I ate a few bites of leftover Japanese last night so I could sleep. If I could just lose twenty pounds, I'd be happy. I used to weigh 112, and now I'm at 165. I feel like a fat ass. But that's a main side effect of pretty much all antipsychotic medications. Michael is really skinny, too, but he said he's up to 135 now, so that's good. I should stop thinking about him before I make myself sick.

Naturally, now I want to take a shower, but I don't have a dry towel. I really need to stop wasting so much water, too. But it feels really nice. Oh, Kim just commented on the photo I just took. She says it's beautiful. It is. Fuck it, I'm going to try to find a dry towel. I need to poop, anyway. I always shower after I poop.

That's better. I didn't have to poop, though. It was just gas. Harry Styles came on the gay playlist for some reason, and it reminded me of his "Sign of the Times" song, so that's what I'm listening to now. I love this song so much. He isn't gay, is he? He's super cute but obviously out of my league. Plus I'm sure he's uncircumcised. I have this horrible discriminatory phobia or dislike of uncircumsized penises. Maybe it's the potential Jew in me. I would still cuddle with him.

I thought this song was about me once. I thought I was the bullet for some reason. But I also thought I was the one he was singing to. I'm so fucked up. I want to get away from here. The end definitely seems near a lot.

The dysphoria is creeping back in. Maybe I should eat a gummy. I didn't have one yesterday at all. I definitely don't feel like drinking any wine, but I need some kind of substance to help numb the pain. The idea of letting a piece of Suboxone dissolve in my mouth makes me want to gag. I found a little piece in one of my pill bottles, though. I'd rather have an actual opiate.

Coldplay is playing. I didn't like them for a long time until I saw them on Tiny Desk with this awesome black choir. They were so fucking good. I was really delusional when I saw it, and I thought they were all CGI animations, though. Regardless, it made me find a new appreciation for their music. I really need to at least clean off my bed. It's fucking nasty. I'm just so damn lazy.

I have a million thoughts happening simultaneously, it seems, in my mind right now. I want to cry. I need a good cry. I don't know how to make myself cry, though. Damn you, Greer. I am so jealous. Seriously. Lights will guide you home and ignite your bones. And I will try to fix you. I need to be fixed. I know I've said that before.

Jeff Buckley's "Hallelujah" is playing now, even though it's a Leonard Cohen cover. Did you know Leonard Cohen wrote like sixty verses or something to this song? He was a genius. This, obviously, reminds me of my delusions of grandeur, which I'll talk about at some point. I think I need an opiate in order to open up about some stuff. I feel like a baffled king. Maybe I'm composing Hallelujah. I don't know if the beauty of a woman will ever overthrow me, though. I do need a haircut. My mom used to cut my hair, but now I just buzz it when it gets too long. I almost always wear a hat, anyway. I have a bad taste in my mouth. I'm going to go brush my teeth again. Oh, wait, I think I have some mouthwash.

Much better. Minty fresh. Band of Horses "Funeral" is on now. I think I wrote that this song reminds me of Cheri and my Uncle Johnny, but that song was actually "Body in a Box" by City and Colour. Both are great songs. I don't know why I just put a "u" in their name. I don't even think they're European or Canadian. Maybe they are. Sometimes I wish I were Canadian.

I just really could use a hug. My whole body hurts, and my mind won't shut the fuck up. I don't mind it when I'm trying to write, but when I'm just sitting there trying to chill out, it gets really fucking annoying. It's non-stop. Maybe I need a lobotomy. They mentioned that on a Golden Girls episode I think. Blah. I'm sad. I want a hot tub or some drugs or a time machine or a cute and nice guy to cuddle me or all of the above.

I'm going to lie down and listen to The Lumineers for a while, I think. Should I eat another gummy? I don't know. They're in Adelaide's room, anyway. She hid them behind the TV so the dogs wouldn't get to them.

Well, I got an email from Paul. He read the first part. He thinks the thoughts and writing are great, but he would love for me to explore each moment in greater detail–like this 30 pages could become 300. That's a lot of fucking pressure. I took another shower. Oh, I actually pooped this time (in the toilet, not the shower). But seriously, what does he mean by that? Lane kind of said the same thing. I can't help how my brain works. Maybe I need some Adderall or meth or something so I won't be so goddamn ADD. Daniel and I were going to make signs when we got out of rehab that said, "Spare attention" because we both have Attention Deficit Disorder. We never went through with it, though, because of crack and all. I still haven't heard back from Daniel. I hope he's okay, even though he's a terrible literary agent so far.

I'm still listening to The Lumineers. They're singing "Ophelia" right now. I think she drowned or something. I don't really remember the myth. I don't really remember a lot of things. That's why my memories are so short, I guess. I just remember certain parts. I guess I could try to tell a long story about one thing. I could be like Stephen King and be super description to an annoyance almost. I've only ever read Misery, but Moses told me some of my life stories remind him of his books–particularly my story about a skeleton key, which I haven't told you yet. That's a pretty stressful story. I'm also the king of digressing, but I will definitely write about it before this book is finished, hopefully. Definitely and hopefully. Sure, whatever. Does that sound arrogant? I'm thirsty, and this Coke is not quenching it for some reason.

I need some drugs to chill me out. I highly doubt a gummy would help, but you never know. My Neurontin should be ready tomorrow. That should help some. It's a nerve blocker. It definitely helps the pain, at least. They give Neurontin to opiate addicts because you can't really get high on it. Although if you take a handful of them every once in a while you can get a slight buzz. That's what I do, anyway.

I'm starting to doubt the rabbi that said alcohol is kosher but marijuana isn't, especially after last night. Alcohol has gotten me into far more trouble than marijuana. I got a DUI a few years ago because these people kept buying me shots in Milledgeville. I fell asleep in my car for a bit, but when I left I forgot to turn on my headlights because it was bright downtown, and I got pulled over. I told them immediately I was drunk, because I was. I probably shouldn't have been driving. Driving on weed is different. I'm extremely careful and utterly paranoid, so I think I do a better job. I wouldn't mind a Xanax or something, even though it would probably make me pass the fuck out.

I was just playing with my booger and pondering about traveling around the country and writing. Maybe that would make this more interesting. It'd be a lot easier if I had more money and if people weren't so paranoid about Covid and all. Maybe I should be more paranoid. Oh well. Maybe I should go back to Georgia. At least then I could possibly obtain some pain pills. That would be swell. I'm going to go ask Adelaide what she thinks.

I'm on the phone with my mom. She's annoying the fuck out of me because I told her I want to come back to Georgia and hang out in Atlanta for a bit, but she's worried I might get killed because "there are some crazy folks in this world these days." She told me to call her back later when my dad is home. If things go as planned (Adelaide was okay with it, by the way–she'll get Timmy to pick up the dog from the vet), I'll be in Atlanta at 3:35 AM, which means I probably won't be able to hang out with Michael. That's okay, though. I'm not even sure if he'd want to hang out with me if he knew what I thought about him last night. The bus leaves Corydon at 4:20 PM, which is my birthday.

She also said I can't take the car more than an hour or so from the house, since the insurance isn't in my name. She is extremely overprotective, but at least she loves me. I didn't think she was my real mother for a while because some random guy from Saudi Arabia messaged me on Facebook and sent me a picture of my friend Tina from Berlin and told me that she was my mother. That was weird. But my dad assures me that he watched me come out of her. Gross.

So two more days until I leave. That's exciting. I hope no one tries to jack my Freewrite while I'm traveling, though. I don't know if I'll be able to transmit my data via Greyhound's WiFi, since there is usually a login screen. I don't think the Freewrite can handle that. That's okay, though. Hopefully it'll be fine. I need to clean up this damn room before I go, even though it wasn't very clean when I got here. I just thought about taking my third shower of the day. The sound of the water is really relaxing, too. I should probably eat something, but I don't feel like it.

Yeah, I took another shower. I also was able to let a quarter of a Suboxone dissolve in my mouth without puking. I feel slightly better. I can't wait to get my Neurontin tomorrow. My stomach feels so empty, by the way. I wish I had some fruit or something. The idea of eating meat right now just grosses me out.

Michael messaged me back. "Sure bro what do you want to do?" I don't think I should get drunk with him. That'd probably be a really bad idea. I'm arriving early in the morning, so maybe we can go get coffee or something. If it's nice weather, we could go to Piedmont Park. That'd be nice. Should I only stay in Atlanta for a few hours? There's a bus I can take to Macon at 1:35. That would give us several hours, assuming there won't be any delays. There are usually delays, though, with Greyhound. I think I'll eat an Italian ice. First I need to put on pants.

I ended up getting an orange push-up instead, since it seems it might have more substance or something. It was good. I really hope nothing too dramatic happens on my journey–nothing bad, at least. Oh, I thought about a picture I want to put on the cover of my book. It's one someone took of Lane and I with our hands in each others' back pockets on the train track at Rose Hill Cemetery in Macon. You can't see our faces, so that's good. Lane is very heterosexual, by the way, but we were really close for a while. He's the one who called me a "no-talent fuck", in case you forgot. He didn't speak to me for a long time because I made a sexual advance through text while I was really methed out years ago. We're okay now, though. I'm glad.

I just remembered that picture is on my bandcamp page. I wonder if I should change the name on there, or at least take down my profile picture, just in case. This is why I need a publisher. They would know what to do. I just don't know if this is really good enough to be published. Maybe people will like reading it while they poop or something.

Sometimes I feel like I'm in a reality show without my knowledge. I've heard that it's called Truman Show Syndrome. Maybe aliens are gods or something are watching me. Who knows?I'm listening to a song I wrote about my grandma. I miss her. She died of brain cancer in 1993. It was a slow, horrible death. She went from being the matriarch of my family to this lifeless, hairless creature drinking food through a straw with her hand down her pants. I've wondered if that's why I'm gay. She was a wonderful woman, though. Everyone loved her. So many people came to her funeral. She bought me my first guitar, but I never played it because it hurt my fingers. I really wanted a CD-ROM drive, even though it probably wouldn't have been compatible with the computer I had at the time. I need a hug. Michael will probably give me one. That'd be cool. It's all just a mystery, can't you see?That was a lyric to the song.

I hate to say it, but I think I might masturbate so I'll feel better for a little bit. I'm just really fucking tense. I came across this really hot midget porn the other day. He was really cute. Who knew? I'll probably watch something different, though. I'd use my own imagination, but my thoughts distract me. I hope I don't feel too guilty afterwards. Once I came upon this web site that said pornography would be a problem for the messiah. This was when I thought I might, unfortunately, be the Jewish messiah. I had my reasons. I'll tell you about them sometime. Meanwhile, I need endorphins desperately.

Okay, I watched "Flirting Fuck Buddies: Theo Brady & Rooney Marx", but I didn't spill my seed. I really like watching black guys fuck white guys for some reason I guess it's the color contrast or something. I don't know. Maybe it's a subconscious racial thing. I was raised to be kind of racist (black people were referred to as "the N-word"), but I grew out of it when I was quite young. My parents wouldn't let any black friends come over to the house, though. Oh, a black boy kissed me in Kindergarten. That was pretty scandalous. I've had sex with a couple black guys. It was okay. One was at The Farm, and one was in the ghetto. He threatened to go get his gun, though, when I told him I had HPV. I didn't let him go anywhere near my butt, though. I'm pretty sure he had it, anyway, after he realized what I was talking about. Oh well. I think he was just pissed that I wouldn't let him fuck me even though I fucked him.

One of my best friends and old roommates was black, but she hasn't talked to me anymore since I was suicidal. She doesn't like it when people are suicidal, apparently. She's kind of famous now because of her music. She was in a band with the son of a really famous country music artist. I would say her name, but I don't want to have to tell her I'm writing about her. I guess I can give her a stage name. Sunny War. I miss her. She really is a great person. I just wish she would talk to me. We used to make tons of money recycling old beer bottles. We drank a lot.

So, here's a decently long story connected to Sunny:

I flew out to LA a couple years ago to hang out with my friend Audrey, who is an artist. I was really high on THC-infused blueberries, and I was having this major debate in my head about what kind of foods were acceptable to eat. Audrey wanted KFC, but I didn't know how to get there. She drew me a map because I had gotten rid of my smartphone since I thought it was the mark of the beast.

But I put the map in my pocket and prayed to God that he would lead my feet to the right kind of food. I walked for a while through Little Armenia and ended up at this Japanese restaurant. I thought it was a little weird that sushi was okay, but that's what I ended up ordering to-go. But as I was about to walk out the door, the lady working pointed to a table and told me to sit. She had laid out this amazing spread of vegetarian dishes and a glass of iced water. It was one of the best and most refreshing meals I'd ever had. I was certain it was a sign.

I left there and continued to pray. I ended up at St. Andrew's, and the Jane's Addiction song popped in my head ("woke up on St. Andrew's), so I stopped to smoke a cigarette. When I looked up, there was this giant construction dumpster across the street with NASA written in giant letters on it. I was sure it was a sign, since I had been thinking a lot lately about how planets might have consciousness (I thought I was quantumly connected to Jupiter, hence the name).

I started praying and walking again. I finally somehow ended up at KFC without using the map. I stood on the corner for a while (no one was around), until this guy on a bicycle came up to me. He told me he thought God had led him to me. And get this: He was wearing a shirt with an astronaut on it that said, "Give me some space!" Crazy.

Then, I finally made it home after talking to him for a while. The sushi was warm by then. Anyway, right as I walked through the door Audrey told me that she had a new client call her and want to commission a painting of Willie Nelson as an astronaut. What the fuck? Sunny was in a band with his son, by the way. That was the connection. But isn't that weird as fuck? Synchronicity, yo.

I'm glad I didn't cum. I don't feel guilty at all. I feel a little better, too, but that's probably due to the Suboxone. I have to pee, but I don't feel like getting up. I'm pretty comfortable. Should I tell Sunny I mentioned her or wait for a lawyer to ask her or whatever if someone picks me up? Fuck it, I have to pee.

I really do miss Sunny. I tried to text her a couple times recently, but she never responded. Sometimes I wonder if it's because she's getting famous or something. I don't know. I heard a song she made recently about Jan, my former street mom and the world's first punk rock DJ. I cried. It was really good. It's called "Memories" if you want to hear it. Wait, "Just Memories". I'm listening to it now. Sad. I miss all kinds of things. Just memories now.

Michael messaged me back. He also had the idea about going to a park. That's cool. I'm excited. I need to call my dad and have him load bus fare onto my card.

Okay, I talked to my mom. She's going to tell my dad to put the money on my card. She also mentioned my medication. She's worried that I might stop taking it, but I haven't. Anyway, so that's cool. I guess this is happening.

Bryan, the guy who was supposed to be my moral compass, just sent me a meme that says, "Suck a cock for Jesus". The idea of sucking a cock right now is not very appealing. I'm so hungry, though. I just don't want to eat. Nothing really sounds appetizing. I'm excited I get to hang out with Michael. I should also call Lucy and let her know. Maybe we can have a little get-together at other Michael's house soon. I need to tell Nicole, too. Maybe I should just tell Facebook. Sometimes I think I overshare on Facebook, though. Well, people tell me I do a lot. I usually end up deleting my posts, though.

Some guy on Grindr just messaged me. He lives close by. He's cute, but no thank you. I have absolutely zero desire to hook up with anyone at all. Maybe I would feel better if I cleaned up this filthy room. I'm going to attempt to do that now.

Okay, I put all the trash in a trash bag along with the mountain of cigarette butts I left in the shower. It looks much better–basically the same as when I arrived. I feel accomplished. I wonder what Paul and Lane mean by wanting to hear more about my stories. Do they mean more detail? What kind of detail? Is my writing unappealing without extra detail? They said they liked it, but I don't want to leave anyone hanging or anything. I'm going to go back and read some of what I wrote.

I read a little bit. It doesn't seem that bad to me. Maybe someone out there will like it. I hope so. I just hope too many people don't like it. The idea of fame is interesting but also very scary. At least I have a pseudonym. I can't believe Paul suggested 300 pages. That's a lot of pages. My fingers are going to fall off. Should that be my goal? How many words are in 300 pages? Maybe it can be a really tiny book or something. That's a good idea. I like the size of The Perks of Being a Wallflower. I wonder if my book is too boring or risque for Penguin. I like penguins. They remind me of Linux, the superior operating system. Oh yeah, I should mention the times I got in trouble for hacking. First I'm going to take another shower because my back hurts. Don't judge.

Shit, I just dropped Timmy's vape, and it fucked up. Adelaide fixed it, though. I'm in her room watching Charmed (the new one) with her. I ate the last gummy that was hidden behind her TV. Oh, and I bought my bus tickets. Michael messaged me and said he can't wait. He says he has days where he really misses me and that he thought about me a few times just today since we talked. That's really sweet. I'm a little high already.

I should stop judging myself so much. I judge myself all the fucking time. It's horrible. Maybe it's right, but it sucks. I should just start doing the right things all the time. That's why I feel like I need a religion to tell me what to do. That would be very convenient. That's one reason I've been drawn to Judaism: they're very legalistic. I actually like that. I wouldn't mind a yoke of fairly-easily-attainable laws. Is that the right word:

attainable? I don't know. I'm high.

I just had a vision of my fantasy coming true. Well, sort of. I had a vision of Michael and his wife asking me to be in a threesome, basically. I highly doubt that would ever actually happen in real life, and even if it did, I might not accept. I don't know. They're married. It just feels wrong, even though they'd both hypothetically be willing partners. It's still adultery, right? I think that's a pretty good question. This is why I need a rabbi on-call. I just want to have a good reason to believe that he's right. Several reasons would be helpful, actually. My eyes just twitched a little for some reason. At one point I thought that happened when God was telling me "no" or something. However, I just misspelled "telling" as "talling", and I wonder if that's because my memory sounds like a tall tale. I am not really sure. I'm kind of high, as I've said. This paragraph feels long, although I can't read the top of it. I wonder how long it is. I wonder what the longest paragraph in the world is. I would Google it, but I don't want to stop typing. I can't stop typing. In high school my keyboarding teacher let me use her truck to go to Subway and smoke cigarettes because I was so good at typing. She was really cool. I wonder if she would approve of this book. I know she's okay with gay people. She was one of the only people who publicly was okay with them when I came out in the 90s. I was probably 16 when it happened. Ok, this run-on paragraph is probably getting too long, so I'm going to end it.

Oh yeah, in my math teacher's class, this girl Amanda Smith found a picture of my boyfriend Brandon in my bookbag and that was around the same time I basically came out. Amanda was my girlfriend in elementary school. I bought her a pink ice ring. She's married now with kids. We hung out exactly once in high school. I rode with her to Dublin for something as she smoked a cigarette out of her sunroof. She's also my third cousin or something, I think. She's also my brother-in-law's cousin. I hope she won't mind me writing about her. I doubt Brandon will care. He's the one who used to be a porn star. He took my v-card.

I'm going to ask them now–well, tell them, really.

I just went to Amanda to ask her on Facebook, and I remembered she never replied to my inquiry about our genealogical connection. She's replying now, though. She says "Lol. Of course. But what about??" I told her it's a meta-memoir. I told her I'm high. She thought she'd have a starring role as my first girlfriend or something. I told her I mentioned that. I told her I'm not writing everything. I'm not. She wasn't aware that we are related. I'm pretty sure we are. Oh yeah, her sister showed up as my 3rd cousin on AncestryDNA.

Cool, Kyle Burgoyne says "That's fine bro" (sic). Kyle is a cool dude. He let me watch him work once. He operates heavy machinery or something. He makes something. I forgot what. But it was neat. I actually got to watch him while I was riding on Greyhound once. What a strange synchronicity. I'm going to send him a picture of my screen like I did to Amanda. This is fun.

I told Animal I was going to make "meta" a trendy term–or that it was going to become one. Has it? I don't know. This was years ago when we were living with Sunny in Inglewood or some shit. Aw, there was this really awesome black chick who used to come hang out with me. Her name is Aarayah. She was cool. I hope she doesn't mind me mentioning her name. I'm going to send her a picture of this. I don't know if she still has the same number. I am high.

Okay, I don't really know if I'll have to change peoples' names, but I hope not. And I hope nothing bad happens if this book gets published. That's the main thing, you know? Fuck. But then again, it'd be cool to have your name in a book. It's not like I'm saying anything bad about anyone, really.

Oh, shit. My friend Jessica just sent me a meme, and I asked her if I could mention the thing she told me about Dr. Roberts in my book. Maybe I should change her name. Did I mention that Adelaide is Dr. Robert's step-sons ex-girlfriend? Anyway, Jessica said I could mention it. He told her that he was working on something "bigger than the Internet" before he died. Dr. Roberts, if you've forgotten, is the inventor of the personal computer. Now I am very nervous. Dr. Roberts was a good man, though. He helped out Greer's dad when he was dying of cancer. Mrs. Rosa really loved him. Mrs. Rosa is a good woman. I'm asking her if it's okay that I mention her. I'm really nervous. It's just part of one of my crazy conspiracy theories, you know. Dr. Roberts was a good man, though. Mrs. Rosa also speaks highly of my mom's side of the family. Maybe I should have the names changed. This is why I need a publishing company–for shit like this. For real, yo. This shit stresses me out. Adelaide thinks it's a good idea to have a legal team and shit. She says the right publisher will come along. Now I am having all kinds of fears. What if someone asks me what I'm writing on my journey? I can always come up with really bad things that can happen. I get that from my mom. And the weed. This is some real, shit though. Fuck. I mean, it may be weird. I don't know. Maybe it's all in my head. I have no idea. Ha. I just read the meme she sent me: "I was so stoned last night… the cops pulled somebody over on T and I ate the joint I was smoking. (sic)" TV, not T. That was my typo that shall be preserved forever. Sorry, editors with OCD. T stands for Tina. Crystal meth. It originally said TV, but yeah. Typos are strange. I like to call them Jungian typos. Carl Jung was fascinated with Euler's number, by the way (which you can derive from the Greek of John 1:1, in case you've forgotten). Shouyld that typo–fuck–be preserved forever? Well now they have to be. Maybe only for this paragraph. Is that a good compromise? Fuck. That was an accident. Embrace the typo. What if I published the whole book without any correction? Fuck correction! You know who needs an editor? People who would get in a death cab. That's who needs an editor.l Ew, that was ugly. That's why we need editors. End preservation.

Maybe I should change my life. Maybe I can write my own life into existence (with possibly the help of God, whoever that may be). I feel bad now for all the fucked up things I've talked about.

Is it okay to say fuck? Do I really need an editor? Fuck. Fuck. Fuck. Fuck. I feel okay, though, for the most part.

Adelaide thinks it's a nice idea to release this unedited as an art project. I think I might get sued into oblivion. Maybe I'll change all the characters' names. That would be a start. That would be a lot of work, though. I want someone else to do it. Let me ask Facebook. I also emailed Wanda and asked her how much she would charge me to do that. She is very professional. I like that. I just don't want to cause any negative feelings. I just happen to have a lot of them. Maybe I should make this fiction. I want to cry. I should heed Adelaide.

Poor Gaga had her dogs kidnapped. Adelaide says when you're famous shit like that happens. I don't want to be famous. I just want to make enough money to get my teeth fixed and have a big party that's not my funeral. I want bad stuff to stop happening. I hate talking about bad stuff. It freaks me the fuck out. Seriously. I'm definitely going to fictionalize this. For sure. I mean, I'm going to change all the names. I just don't anyone to get hurt because of me, including me. I definitely need an editor. I hope I can get Wanda to be my editor. Or if she doesn't want to do it, I hope someone else will want to. Maybe I should do it. Why not? Adelaide agrees. She thinks I'm right to change the names. She says to change them when I'm done. I don't have to do it right now. Adelaide said a bunch more stuff, but I forget what because I am very high. Fuck it. All that fretting was for nothing. That's what the TV just said. Adelaide's watching Meateater on Netflix. I don't know if I want to know what this is about. Meat isn't murder but it's definitely similar. Well, I guess it depends on your definition of "murder". Okay, I don't want to turn my life into a fucking thriller, although I'm used to it for sure. For sure for sure. You couldn't even imagine. Most people think I'm crazy. Maybe I am. This is an exercise of free will. That's what I just decided. I think things should just be redacted and shit like I've been doing. You can't squeeze blood out of a turnip. But I'm not a turnip. Fuck that. Maybe that's why I've had my blood drawn so many fucking times. For a while I thought they were vampires at the hospital. The nurse's last name was Stackhouse or some shit. It reminded me of that show. And the doctors and nurses licked their lips as they slowly backed out of the room after I started humming Alanis Morisette's "Uninvited". I thought my therapist Joseph Smith was one of them. Actually I thought he was a Nephilim. He said something about me having tens of thousands of thoughts per day like him. Do all people experience that? He says I'm one of his favorite people to talk to. Talking about this is making me extremely paranoid. And my battery is low. Fuck. I need a charger, but it's upstairs, and I'm lazy. I'm pretty sure they're killing ducks or something on this show. I like ducks, even though they're rapists with razor blade feet. I was telling Adelaide that dolphis (Jungian typo, maybe) were rapists, too, and she got really excited about the fact that they can breathe underwater. I was telling her how ducks will hold their victim-partner's head underwater when they apparently rape them. Fuck, I need a real cigarette. This vape ain't cuttin' it. That's how I really talk. Just kidding. Not really. Well, I talked more like that when I was like fourteen because there's a video of me when we were redoing my nephew's baby room or whatever, and he was born in 1995. So I guess it was 1995. I had a really southern accent in it. I was probably 13. I also sounded pretty gay. Oh, I made a video of me jerking off on tape and gave it to someone. I was 15 then, though. That's a little different from 13, I think. A little. Adelaide just said something that synced weirdly with what I was thinking, but I forgot what. I just realized that writing on a Freewrite is way better than thinking to yourself constantly. Finally, maybe someone will sort of understand what it's like to have my fucked up brain. I have to pee, thankfully, because I was thinking of something I was too afraid to say.

Okay, I decided I'm going to change everyone's name except for celebrities. Adelaide agrees that it's a good idea. Dr. Roberts is a celebrity, but not Mrs. Rosa. I'll change all the names when I'm done or get a publisher to do it. Maybe I should ask the New York Post. Traci tried to get me to leak a story to them once, but my mom wouldn't let me. I have no idea what the story was about. I told Adelaide I have a whole smattering of D-list celebrities to talk about. She laughed at my word choice. She told me to keep it interesting. Fuck, I just fixed a possibly Jungian typo. There was a number 4 in the middle of the word "interesting". What does that mean? Fuck typos. Or are they existential clues? I wish Wanda would email me back. Oh well. I already changed her name. I just sent Ms. Rosa another message to tell her I could change her name, but I don't know that changing Dr. Roberts's name will have any effect other than the confusing grammar relating to possessive words that end in "s".

My mom always tells me that people are afraid of what they don't understand. That's why people are afraid of me. That's what she thinks, anyway. People have definitely been afraid of me before. I've never hurt anyone, although I did try to defend myself when my dad was beating the fuck out of me last year. He says it was the worst thing he'd ever done in his life. He just had a lot of built-up animosity, I guess. I still care for him. He's been working on a camper van he bought for a long time. He got it after Josh died. The reason he was beating the shit out of me was because I told him if he touched me I'd fucking kill him. He said, "Well Kill me then!" and started wailing on me. He gave me a black eye and tons of knots on my head, and I broke my pinky trying to shield my face. I feel like I've fucked myself in the realm of anonymity since I've told so many people I'm writing this book. I've told a few people what my pen name is, but yeah. Who knows? I need professionals. For sure. I don't know. I freaked out worrying about it, and Adelaide said to just figure it out as I go along. That's what I'll do. I'll go wherever God or the Universe takes me. I like that Catholics are called universal. It kind of goes with my planetary consciousness hypothesis.

What if, what if, what if, what if. So many "what ifs". It gets absurd. I sometimes feel like my server's probability drive is broken. My eyes just twitched again. I guess that's a "no". I haven't talked much about the "yes" version, have I? I'll save that for later. I just thought of something else that I probably shouldn't tell you. Some things just shouldn't be told. I could go on, but I won't. Do you think I have a large ego? Sometimes I think I do. It's not like something I'm trying to have or anything. Like. Like. Like. Like. Like. Like. Like. Like. Like. Like. Like. Like. Like. Like. Like. Like. Like. Like. Like. Sorry, just trying to make up for all the missing "likes" for previous whatever. I don't know. I'm high. I forgot where I was going with that, and I don't feel like reading. I keep coming up with brilliant ideas for TV shows, but I space out and forget to type until after they've moved on like clouds off the sides of the screen. I should definitely change the names. Onomatopoeia. That was just a bookmark so I can remind myself of something that I already forgot. My brain won't shut the fuck up. I need a real cigarette. NOW.

I feel a little better. Adelaide and I talked for a bit, and she said some stuff that I already forgot. She's eating cereal, and it looks pretty good. Krave chocolate chip cookie dough by Kellogg's.

I feel a lot better. I ate some cereal. It was really good. I also decided I need an editor. But then again, what if the typos really are Jungian? This is becoming a fucked up book. Oh well. I just thought about how I used to fart in times like these and say, "That's what I think about that." I'd do it right now but I don't have any gas, and I don't know if Adelaide would mind. Timmy farts all the time, apparently, though. She wants to know if he's trying to shoot a turkey or a bear or something. She's talking to the TV I think.

I kind of feel bad that I've said bad things about my family right after my mom told me not to. Maybe I should edit those parts out. Abigail just said something that seemed to be synchronic with that, but I forgot what it was. Wait, Abigail isn't her name. I should definitely edit out this paragraph. Onomatopoeia.

This is turning into a shit show. Makes me want to have another real cigarette. Abigail said I can call her either Adelaide or Abigail. So that's cool. Ugh, I just had a rotten tooth taste in my mouth. I really need to go to the dentist. I went the other day, but since I'm going back to Georgia I'll have to go to one there. I know a good man who makes partials for cheap. That's probably what I'll end up getting until I can miraculously afford implants.

Abigail says her face is burning because of the tanning bed. That sucks. I could use some Vitamin D and maybe a tan. I wanted to go down to Miami and go to restaurant row, maybe stay at the Four Seasons. I love the Four Seasons. They watch for you to start coming back to your room and have a delicious snack like fish dip and plantains waiting on you. And they give you frozen grapes on the beach. I don't mind being pampered every once in a while. I hate pedicures, though. Fuck that. My rich Jewish friend, Haley, and I spent like $10k in a week at the Four Seasons. I should really call her by her name, but it's becoming like a running gag or something, at least in my mind. This thing has been saying "battery low" for a while. I wonder how many words I've written today. Eric's half-brother suggested I write a minimum of 25k words per week after I said I'd write 5k-10k words per day. I started working Friday on Purim, and now it's Tuesday. So that's like five days. I've written 39,241 words total. I can't operate a calculator, apparently,well enough to tell you how many words that is per day. It's almost 40k, though. Is it a turn-off for me to write about word count? Does it stress you out that you have read this much? That's only like half-way through an average book, I think.

Oh, did I mention that I got a reply from the number I thought belonged to the cool black chick in Inglewood or whatever? I had the wrong number. Oh well.

I don't think this book knows where it's going, even though so far it has told nothing but the truth from the author's perspective, at least. I don't claim to know the capital-T Truth– not for sure, at least. I'm reminded of my friend Zero because I accidentally typed at 0 that I erased. I lived with him in Boyle

Heights. He has signatures of directors and shit all over his arms and kind of looks like his dog. I'm definitely going to have to change his name, even though it's a cool name that he gave himself, legally. Adelaide said "Eww" out loud as I was typing that. She's not reading what I'm writing, though. Although I did think she had read some when she asked me if I was okay earlier in the kitchen. I'm hungry. I don't want my hamburger, though. It tastes too much like an animal. Yay, I forgot about the cereal! Adelaide handed it to me so I didn't even have to get up.

I was just thinking about Amanda as I was munching, no lesbian pun intended. Does anyone even care? Am I trans? Probably not, but I don't know. For some reason I feel like I might be more likely to hook up with a girl if I had a vag. I don't know why. I hope it's not because of a fucked up Oedipus thing. I don't want my brain to even go there.

Paul just emailed me back. I'm back upstairs in my room– Adelaide was tired. He said I should explore everything I wrote about in Part One more. He said to describe the places and smells and how one person reminds me of something. He said to keep writing what I'm writing but to "expand the universe" if I want to review one day. He wants me to show the entire iceberg instead of the tip. He did say it was wonderful, though. Or maybe he was talking about the iceberg. The tip reminds me of uncircumsized penises. The smell is probably pretty cheesy or something. A place I experienced once was in one of my ex-boyfriends' bedrooms. We used "fish" as a code-word for "I love you." His penis didn't smell, though, I don't think. His name was Michael, too. He was really cute and nice. I forgot why we broke up. I've dated a lot of people. I don't really smell much right now–probably because I chain-smoke cigarettes. I don't usually remember smells except for my grandma's Oil of Olay night cream and lots of foods. I don't want to say what that reminds me of because it's about my family, and I'm not supposed to talk bad about my family.

Paul's email says it was sent from the future. Maybe he's right.

Maybe it was or will be. I don't even know that it's even an iceberg and not a giant whale wanting to swallow me whole. Not everyone can smell, anyway. I should have this published in braille. I just remembered the smell of semen, which is connected to a memory of Paul wanting me to leave some of mine on a shirt for him. I did. He obtained my DNA.

I feel boring now. I'm going to take a shower.

Okay, it's whatever. I listened to "23" by Blonde Redhead and felt better. Now a song called "Oh Mandy" by The Spinto Band is playing. I'm reminded of my friend Mandy, of course. I should send her a message. I haven't talked to her in a while, although I feel like I already have too many characters in this book. I like her, though. She reads tarot, gives massages, drinks wine, and likes Tori Amos. Once she gave me this amazing energy healing or something. I ended up passing out on the massage table. I feel like my book is boring now. I'm sorry if my mind is boring you, but this is experimental art, so go fuck yourself if you don't approve. I think Paul just thinks in terms of movies. I get that, but I'm not trying to make a movie. I'm just downloading the contents of my mind, which rarely includes smells or scenery detail. I hate this fucking planet. I am a no-talent fuck. Fuck.

I don't even want to type anymore. I'm going to find something to watch and numb my brain.

Nevermind. I found this gay movie, but I couldn't fall asleep. I'm wide awake, really. It's only like 12:30. This movie is pretty damn cheesy. If they can do it, so can I—not that I want to make a movie or think this could somehow be a movie. My mind started fantasizing about Michael again, but I stopped myself. I just had a fleeting urge to take a shower, but I picked my nose instead. I guess this could be a really complicated TV show with a fuckton of characters, but I don't want to write that. I'd be on a committee or something, maybe. I still wish I had someone in my bed. I'm so lonely or something. I don't really know what it is. I feel... disconnected. Oh, I forgot to tell you about getting in trouble for hacking, although it wasn't a huge deal. It wasn't even really hacking, in my opinion, even though I got banned from my ISP the first time and ISS the second time. They even put a rule in the school rule book because of it. It's really nothing. I just found some credit card numbers and final exam answers. I was just trying to impress a cute Senior for the latter. The first one was just from plundering an FTP server. Sorry if that's not descriptive enough, but it is what it is. That phrase reminds me of Traci Nobles. She said that on TV after the news broke about Anthony Weiner's leaked nudes. That had nothing to do with me, though, even though I had them. That was weird. I miss Traci. I had such a crush on her when we were little kids. Why the fuck am I gay?

God, this movie is so lame. They're singing in it, which is making it awkward. It's not horrible–just cheesy. I won't say what it's called. That would be mean. I hope Michael gives me a great hug. I know he will. Fuck I'm pathetic. Just be thankful you're not me. It really sucks being me. I definitely wouldn't recommend it. It's pretty painful in every way. I'm so fucked up.

I need help. I need something. I feel like I'm missing something huge. I wish God were real. Maybe he or she is. Suicidal thoughts have started to come. Maybe I should check myself into a psych ward again. No, that's stupid. I'm going back to Georgia in two days. Maybe I need to have my meds changed. I just feel so dirty and empty and alone. I want to be a baby. I want to be in a womb. I literally wish I had never been born. This world is kind of horrible. I am kind of horrible. Sometimes I slap myself really hard because I just hate the fuck out of myself. I don't have the energy for that right now. Maybe I'll take another shower. Some dirt just can't be washed away, though.

I took a shower and felt slightly better. I guess I should have told you that right before I wrote that last paragraph, I finished the movie and ended up masturbating to completion. I just want to stop doing bad things, but first I need to figure out what's bad. Why can't I just be fixed? Maybe I should just let a therapist or psychologist read this. I'd much prefer help over fame or fortune anyday. I'll just go back to school and finish my Social Work degree and help people. I want to be good. I want to feel complete–either that, or I want to stop existing.

I don't know if my brain can learn a new language. A rabbi told me I needed to learn Hebrew. Maybe Christianity or something is right though–at least some flavor of it. I don't know. I think I mentioned before the equation through which you can derive pi, Euler's number, and alpha (the fine structure constant) from Genesis 1:1 and John 1:1. You just have to multiply the number of letters by the product of letters and divide by the number of words times the product of words. If you do that, you get pi and e, respectively, to five accurate digits each. If you concatenate and square the sums, you get alpha to five significant digits. That just can't be a coincidence.

Genesis 1:1 speaks about the creation of the heavens and the Earth, both of which are generally spherical, which makes pi significant. John 1:1 speaks about the Logos or Word or Light, which makes the derived euler's number significant since it is used in calculations of waveforms and compounding interest (savings). I need a savior. Jesus claimed to be the Word made flesh. I think the Word may be the Torah. He could've been a walking Torah, although probably most Jews would disagree. I wonder if my Jewish therapist will read this. He might charge me. I don't know. I just really, really need help. Meanwhile, I have got to find something to distract me. My mind won't shut up. It's horrible. Please help me. No one can hear me. I miss Josh. Why did he have to die? Why does everyone have to die but me? I had so much comfort with him. June 3, 2018. It seems just like yesterday. Everything is so messed up. I miss my grandma. At least my mom is still here. I don't know what I'll do if she goes before me. I'll be so lost. I'm already lost enough. I can't tell her how I'm feeling, though, because she'll get upset. It sucks. I need to take my meds. I'm going to go watch a movie until I pass out.

CHAPTER X

I don't even know what to say. I should probably lay off the drugs, even weed. Weed is a drug. I know some people call it a medicine or whatever, but medicines are drugs. Did you know the Greek word for sorcery is pharmakeia? That's where the word pharmaceuticals comes from, at least. In the Book of Revelation it says that the nations will be deceived through the use of pharmakeia. Maybe I should be deceived, though. I probably have too much shit in my head as it is.

I'm leaving tomorrow. I'm a little nervous. I hope I'm doing the right thing, if there is such a thing. No one's going to want to publish this monstrosity. What am I even doing? Oh, yeah, I'm going to give it to a psychologist. I just don't know any psychologists. Well, Alli is a child psychologist, I think. She's the one from IRC who gave me the roses. I guess I could ask her. I just realized she didn't reply to the last email I sent her about hating the world. Maybe she just didn't know how to respond. That's usually the excuse when people don't respond to me, which happens often.

I'm watching some lady doing scrapbook shit on YouTube. I like her voice. It's soothing. I would mention her name, but I wouldn't want to embarrass her. She seems really wholesome, even though she just mentioned how she hates it when people drive slowly in the fast lane. I should probably stop judging people, though. I think I'm going to lie down again, even though it's past two. I hope I can sleep on the bus some tomorrow before I get to Atlanta.

Okay, I took a shower (to get clean) and ate half a bowl of Frosted

Flakes because my stomach felt too empty. It still does, but not as bad. I'm really mesmerized by this scrapbooking video. My sister scrapbooked for a while. She's a nurse. She is fairly wholesome. I'm definitely the black sheep. I'm going to lie down again.

Well, I ended up going to pick up my prescription at Walmart in Corydon. I saw a dead horse on the way. I was going to tell the possible owners, but their driveway was blocked off with cinder blocks for some reason. Other than that, the drive was beautiful. It's a lovely day, and the scenic route is always nice. I ended up taking three Neurontin, even though I'm only supposed to take one. But I'm a drug addict. I can't help it. Plus it usually takes more than one for it to do anything. I petted Itchy for a while after I pooped. He's lounging in the desk chair. The scrapbooking lady is still talking. It's kind of hot in my room now. I'm going to miss this place. Oh, Adelaide's dad told her he really liked me. I really like him, too. He's a good dad.

Alli said I should start calling people from Psychology Today. It's a bitch trying to find someone who takes my insurance, though. It'll probably be even harder to find someone who'd also be willing to read this shit. Oh well.

Michael asked me if I've ever tried shrooms. I have. Jailbird Timmy, Opey, and I used to get them from a cow field by the river in Milledgeville. I eventually found out the land belonged to my friend Judi's sister. She died. She was cool–the only person I've ever known who could really handle her meth. I don't know if I want to try shrooms again, though. I don't know if my brain could handle it. I think I hit 42,000 words. Forty-two is one of my favorite numbers. I already told you that. It's probably a lot of people's favorite number. Alpha is still cooler. Oops, that's the number that Carl Jung was obsessed with–not Euler's number. My bad.

Michael asked me if I wanted to smoke a wake and bake joint and watch the sunrise at Piedmont or Olympic Park since I'll be arriving early. I just hope I don't get delayed anywhere. That sounds nice, even though I was going to stop using THC for a while. Oh well. Oh, cool, he's going to bring his singing bowls so we can do some meditation. I suck at meditation, though. My mind never shuts up. I do like singing bowls, though. I feel bad I kind of objectified him.

I just played a song I wrote on my ukulele. Singing makes me feel better. This guy Brooke just posted on Facebook that he charges $100 to record, mix, and master a song. I'm thinking about getting him to do it for me once I get my stimulus check, although I've had several other people offer. It just hasn't happened yet. His ex-wife was briefly famous for performing with some famous Swedish band or something when she was like fourteen. I hung out with them at the Huddle House once. I think we had a pretty good conversation. I had a crush on Brooke for a while, but I'm over it. Fucking straight guys. Brooke has really good taste in music–mostly 90s stuff, though. I miss the 90s.

I'm watching this pretty cute gay movie called The 10 Year Plan. There's a scene where they go to Chi Chi Larue's sex store. I went to dinner with her once. Bruce Vilanche, the famous comedian with red glasses, was there, too. That was when I lived with all the porn stars in Huntington Beach. I got invited to a party at Brian Singer's house in Palm Springs, but I didn't go. That was before people started calling him a kiddie diddler or whatever. The porn director I was staying with, who also used to manage Dusty Springfield, was interviewed on some gay web site about it. I can't remember what he said, but I think he called him a predator or something. I never met the guy, though, I don't think.

This movie is making me want a husband. I wouldn't mind having a normal life. I think I'd be a pretty good housewife–with the right medicine, at least. I really need to take this pink fingernail polish off my pinky so no one will want to beat me up on the bus tomorrow. I also need to do laundry and throw this trash bag away. There are ashes everywhere, too, which I need to get rid of. I also should eat something, but nothing sounds appealing. I really hope I can get some sleep on the bus tomorrow before I hang out with Michael. I always feel cracked out when I don't sleep. This movie also makes me want an extra dirty martini. I used to order them at Applebee's in Dublin. We called them "Christini Martinis"–dirty like Christina Aguilera. I love olives. That sounds really good right now. I also really like their boneless wings and perfect margaritas. Yum. I'm so hungry. I just don't want to eat any meat. Well, fast food would be good. I should've picked up something in Corydon. Oh well.

Wow, the ending to that movie was really good. It made me cry. I wish I could have love like that, but my love life has been pretty tragic. I don't know if there's any hope for me. I'm going to go do laundry now.

Adelaide just got home from work. She told me she'd take me anywhere I want to eat, so P chose this fancy restaurant in Corydon called 1815. Their menu looks really good. I'm pretty excited and starving.

1816. That's the name. That's the year Corydon became the state capital of Indiana, which didn't last long according to the super cute waiter. I wrote that he was cute on my receipt. Well, at least the part that wasn't covered by a mask was cute. I liked his personality, too. Oh, this older gentleman and I had a conversation about the Fibonnaci sequence. That was neat. Adelaide had fried green tomatoes, and I had the crab cakes. It was the most expensive item on the menu but worth every penny. We're going to go watch a movie now. I'm not sure what.

Ok, we're watching It's Kind of a Funny Story. It's pretty good, although I'm not paying much attention. Adelaide is and keeps giving me updates if I leave the room. Chaz, my ex (the one whose popsicle stick house I tore down), messaged me on Facebook. He said it was okay that I wrote about him. He remembers the day we drove to the middle of nowhere when I was going through withdrawals and decided I needed to walk around in nature. That was the first time he ever saw a bear. That was a good day. Chaz is such a cutie, but I never wanted to have sex with him while we were together because I was strung out on opiates. That's basically why we ended up breaking up, I guess. I don't know. His perspective may be different.

Oh, I ate two small squares of weed chocolate, but I don't think it has kicked in yet. I don't think I'll be taking my candy with me on the bus, but maybe someone will be able to enjoy them at some point. This movie has a decent depiction of a psychiatric hospital, although from my experience it's hit or miss whether or not you'll have a good time.

I was just telling Adelaide about the time I spent at Peachford. That's where I met Michael. I actually went there after I left Indiana the last time. Anyway, before I met Michael, there was this guy in there who I thought was really cute. He was only nineteen, though. We ended up being roommates in the outpatient program. One day some people were fighting, and I got scared, so he cuddled me on my bed to comfort me.

I ended up giving him a blow job. He came in like two minutes. He wouldn't kiss me, though, since he was supposedly straight. He did talk about going on an adventure with me in my camper van. But then he started avoiding me–he wouldn't even sit with me in the cafeteria. I wanted to leave, and when the Director asked me why, I told her I was a love addict, and I told her what happened. Apparently she told him what I said, and he accused me of rape. The cops came and interviewed me and everything. Of course everyone knew I wasn't a rapist. But he was Muslim, so maybe that had something to do with it. I don't know. But it really hurt my feelings. I really liked him. Anyway, they ended up sticking me back in the main building for a while, and that's where I met Michael. So I'm kind of thankful that it happened, I guess. Oh yeah, I told everyone he had a freckle on his dick (on the underside) because how would I know that if I had raped him? You can't rape the willing. It really fucking sucks to be accused of that, by the way.

I was going to have Adelaide write something, but she accidentally erased everything. She was going to say that the keys remind her of the computer she used to write a short story on at summer camp when she was a kid. I am in love with my Freewrite. The keys are so clicky and awesome. Thank you, Astrohaus. Okay, Adelaide said she also would have written, "My own vagina has betrayed me". I'm not entirely sure why she said that, but she did. Oh, she said her vagina prefers Timmy over her. She felt guilty about having an orgasm by herself yesterday. I guess that's what she's talking about.

Let's see, I started writing on Purim, which was Friday. Today's Wednesday, so that's five days. I was going to write a week's worth of thoughts, which means this book would end after I hang out with Michael. That's kind of sad. I can always write more, though, if anyone wants me to. I don't mind writing. It's probably therapeutic or something. I need to start packing. First I'm going to take a shower because I feel a little weird and unclean since I spilled my seed during an intermission. I have little self-control.

I'm going to see if I can make myself go to sleep early so I can sleep on the bus tomorrow.

Nevermind. I can't. I was watching this guy test out fountain pens on YouTube, which is very calming, but I'm just not that sleepy. I posted on Reddit asking for tips on finding a publishing company, but I haven't gotten any replies yet. I always have terrible luck on Reddit. A lot of people there are just assholes. What am I even doing? Are there people who will really like reading this? Maybe I should talk about famous people more. Um, my friend Amanda Newman's uncle is friends with Prince Edward, but I don't have any gossip about him. I was there when Patty Duke got her star in Hollywood. Her sons are pretty cute. One was in The Magicians, and the other one was in Lord of the Rings. I don't know any of these people, though. Oh, I hung out with some Warhol Superstars at my friend's birthday party once. Mary Waranov is cool. They joked about how they hadn't done coke since the 80s. It was an okay party. And Jimmy Carter is my 5th cousin. That's lame. I think I already mentioned him, anyway. I was going to say, "fuck celebrities", but that sounds mean. Really, though, I don't do well with famous people, really. I don't know why. I don't really know if I would want to be famous or not. I'd like to maybe have a taste of it for a little bit or something. I'd like the nice restaurants, fancy hotels, clothes, and parties that come with it, though. That'd be cool, although I don't know if that happens anymore to authors. My great-grandfather's name was Arthur. He died from a bad liver. I have a bad liver, too. It's in my DNA report, and I had kidney stones a couple years ago. Wait, kidneys not liver. He had bad kidneys. Kidney stones are the worst. I do not recommend it. I'm going to take another shower now. My Reddit post got down-voted, by the way. Fuck them. Oh, wait, no, that was the first one that was removed because it wasn't formatted right. Nevermind. Shower.

Ok, I think I'm high. I'm watching the cast of The Magicians chat on Zoom. This hardly has any views. That's crazy. The Magicians are amazing. I'm high. Should I self-publish? I don't know. I don't even know if anyone will want to read this dribble. I'm going to need an editor, and I can't afford one. But it'd probably really annoy people with OCD if I don't edit it. That would suck. I want to hang out with this cast. They all seem super cool. I don't want to have to be famous, though. I just want to hang out with famous people, even though a lot of them can be dicks. But who can't? Fuck. I'm high. I'm going to try to call Moses.

Okay, I talked to him for a long time. I finally decided I'm going to leave this unedited and self-publish. I'm just going to run spell check, but all the remaining typos are Jungian typos and part of the Synchronicity because that is what is probably true. Maybe even True. Jungian slip. That's what they're called. Fuck Reddit.

Goddamnit, Quentin and what's-her-face, oh Julia, from The Magicians were just talking about being homeless for the night to help the homeless youth. I miss being homeless. That was one of the best times of my life. I was so fucking happy. I hate this world. I hate most of the people, especially the ones who use Reddit. They're the absolute worst, I think. Fuck the Internet. Goddamn Beast of Revelation. Fuck. I need a hug. I want to cry, but I can't. I miss Greer, even though we don't hug each other. That's like, our thing. I need something to knock myself out. Everything is bullshit. I hate life. Oh yea, someone left a really long comment on my Reddit post telling me I had to edit, edit, edit, and they made me feel really pretentious. But I don't know if they're right or if they're an asshole or both. I don't know what's going to happen next. I just don't know. Good night, hopefully.

CHAPTER XI

Well, I'm at the bus station, which is actually a Burger King. I ate some onion rings with Zesty sauce, but my cheeseburger almost made me puke. I had to spit it back out into my bag. Adelaide's dad gave me his old newsboy cap before I left, and Adelaide gave me $10 in case I needed to buy snacks. They are such good people. I'm going to miss them and Samson and Itchy and all the animals–even Timmy.

It's 1:26, and my bus doesn't leave until 4:20. There's a Goodwill and Waffle House next door, but I don't feel like lugging my suitcase around. There's a hearse parked in the Goodwill parking lot. That's pretty strange. I wonder if someone from there drives it, or maybe it was a donation. Can you donate vehicles to Goodwill? I hope this isn't foreshadowing something. I don't want to die in my book or in real life yet. Moses wrote about his own death, though, supposedly, according to people who think he wrote the Torah–or maybe someone else did. I don't know. I kind of would like to see my Moses, but there's no way my mom will let me take my car all the way to Tallahassee. I wish I could take a nap, but I don't know if the employees would like that. Maybe I'll be able to sleep on the bus.

I got a few comments on my Reddit post. Most of them–well, all of them, really–are pretty critical. Someone said I might come across as "puffed up". I've obsessed over the fact that I might have too much pride over the years. My mom's cousin said King David's sin was pride. I don't know what to do about it, though. I don't know how to humble myself, although I've prayed for it a lot. Someone did mention doing a writing workshop, which sounds pretty appealing. I just hope I can find a free one. I told

Paul I feel like this is futile, but he told me he wants more.

The employees here are really nice. One of them just told me where the bus would come so I could watch out for it. I'm going to be here for a while, though. I think I'm going to call Nicole. She doesn't know I'm coming home, yet. I only have 23% battery life on my phone, though, and the nearest outlet is pretty far away. She didn't answer anyway. I'll call my mom.

My mom kind of sounded fucked up a little. They changed her medication, and I guess that's a side effect. I hope everything goes okay for a while, at least, living with them again. I don't even know how many times I've been kicked out. It's ridiculous.

The first time was when I was seventeen, I think. My dad had just been diagnosed with PTSD, and he had to file bankruptcy. He lost his company and the house I grew up in. It was my Senior year, and they were planning on moving to Dublin. I wanted to stay in our house until it was sold, but they wouldn't let me. It's kind of a blur what happened, but I guess I pitched a fit. I went into my room and locked the door, but my dad beat it down. Then he brought a shotgun into my room and kneeled at the end of my bed, saying something about killing himself. I think my mom finally got him to leave, and I climbed out the window and ran barefoot all the way to my aunt's house. I ended up staying with my sister for a while. I remember listening to Sarah Mclachlan's album all night and crying. The last instrumental track is one of my favorites. I really like the sound of the saw–or maybe it was something else. I don't know. Fuck, robots keep blowing up my phone. That's so annoying.

So what's the iceberg, really? All I can think about is lettuce. I'm drawing a blank. Is this writer's block or just trepidation or something? Did I use that word correctly? Maybe I do need to edit. I need an editor, but I can't afford Wanda. My friend Zero mentioned something about a Wanda on Facebook being a villain, and it kind of creeped me out. I don't want Wanda to be a villain. She's not. She's cool. I'm just a broke ass bastard.

I'm going to go smoke a cigarette. I don't want to annoy the employees by going in and out all the time, but I guess they're used to it since this is a fast food restaurant.

That's better. Fuck, I'm so impatient. That is another one of my flaws. Although I'm definitely resilient. When I'm in a psychiatric hospital and they ask us for a good quality about ourselves, that's what I always say. I haven't even told you about some of the most fucked up things that have happened to me. It's hard to describe some of it, and it stressed me out to think about it. I'll try to tell you about it before the end, but I hope it's not anti-climactic or something. If this is going to only last a week, I need to start getting it out. Maybe I will on the bus.

I just talked to my sister for a bit on the phone. She says I can mention her, as long as it's something good. She said my niece is in Atlanta right now at some conference for school. She wants to be an ultrasound technician. That's pretty cool. I'm proud of her.

I don't really have many bad memories involving my sister. When I was little I used to pretend to put makeup on her as she fell asleep. I think she just liked me rubbing her face. And when her boyfriends would come over, I was kind of a brat to them. Once I also ran a vacuum cleaner hose from her door to the living room so everyone could hear what she was saying when she was on the phone. She's almost ten years older than me, so I guess she's more of an aunt than a sister–or at least, she was when I was little.

Wow, I got downvoted to Hell on Reddit. I didn't even post any of my writing. People are on there are such dicks. It definitely seems like a hive mind sometimes. I think I'm going to run spell check on the last part now.

The bus was supposed to be here at 4:00, but it's 4:08, and it hasn't come yet. I hope I won't be late for my transfer in Louisville. I chatted with several people since I last wrote, but I don't want to bore you. I did talk to this black girl I went to highschool with about racism, so that was cool. I was telling her how my family is a lot less racist now because I always get onto them. Is my book boring? That would mean that my thoughts are boring, since that's basically all that it contains. I really hope the bus hurries up. It's supposed to leave at 4:20, so there's still time. My phone is down to 15%. I have to go pee. I'm outside, and I hope no one jacks my shit.

Alright, I made it quick. Where the fuck is the bus? I'm starting to get nervous. I don't know if I ever had a bus that was on time, though. Maybe I should call the company. Holy shit, Greyhound's intro message on the phone is long as shit. I hate talking to robots. Okay, I'm on the phone with the bus company that's taking me to Louisville. I've been on hold for a while. Maybe I should've flown, but it's too late now. I flew up here, but I thought it would be more interesting to take the bus back. I'm regretting my choices. Okay, cool, the guy said it'll be here in five minutes. That's a relief.

Oh wait, I think he said twenty-five minutes. He said the bus was at the Magnolia exit, which is twenty-five minutes away. I should still be able to make it to my Atlanta bus on time, though. It doesn't board until 6:40. I asked Adelaide's ex in Louisville if he wanted to hang out, but he hasn't seen the message. She thinks I should hook up with him, but he secretly prefers black twinks. He's cute, though. Oh wait, I keep forgetting this is supposed to be a memoir. Damn, I forgot to take off my nail polish.

I just checked out someone with pink hair, but I think it might've been a girl. That reminds me of the time I was at this underground party in NYC. This guy, who wasn't really my type physically, started dancing with me, and I was really attracted to him. Then I found out he was a transman. I'm pretty sure it was the testosterone or something that did it for me. I find a lot of trans men attractive, but I don't know how my peepee would feel about their lack of a peepee. I've only put my pee pee in a vajayjay once, and that was at this Air Force toga party while I was making out with this hot supposedly straight guy. He wanted to see it. I pushed her off after a few seconds because it was entirely too weird. I don't want to think about it. I get the concept, though, of how it could feel good physically. But mentally, it's just not for me. Anyway, I'm going to smoke one more cigarette before the bus gets here, even though I only have five left.

God fucking damn it. Never use Miller Trailways. They were supposed to be here at 4:00 with boarding at 4:20. They got here like 30 minutes late, and the driver didn't even pull into the Burger King parking lot. I was getting my things together, and he left me. He wasn't even here for a minute.

I was so livid. I've calmed down a little now, though. I think I'm just going to fly. Fuck it. There are two flights from Louisville tomorrow. One arrives in Atlanta at 7 in the morning and one at 5:30 in the afternoon. I'm waiting on a response from Michael to see what he thinks I should do. I'm going to go ahead and try to get a refund from Greyhound. They better give me one. That was ridiculous. I have a feeling that they won't give me one since I didn't have a "flexible ticket". Evil fucking bastards. Maybe this is a sign. I hope it isn't. I can't believe that asshole driver left me.

Well, I texted Michael an hour ago, and I still haven't heard back from him. I don't know if I should go ahead and buy a ticket before it's too late or what. Adelaide should be here soon. My phone is at 2%. This sucks. Why is this happening to me? I have the worst luck. Or maybe it's God or the Universe or whatever trying to tell me something. Maybe I shouldn't hang out with Michael. I really want to, though. I just don't know.

Okay, he just texted back. He says I can't crash with him because he only has one bedroom. I want to kill myself. Well, I just feel like a stupid piece of shit. I don't know what to do. I wish I could just stop existing. Adelaide just got here, but she's getting something to eat.

Well, we're back at the house. I took a shower and then jerked off to a porn of a really hot guy with full body tattoos getting fucked by a transgirl. I feel better, even though a good cry would've been preferable. Adelaide told me I should finish my bottle of wine, so that's what I'm doing. I told her on the way back that it feels like there's a god who hates me. Maybe it's because I'm a fag. Maybe God really does hate fags. I don't know. I just know that I'm fucked up. Existence is hard. I don't like it at all sometimes. Anyway, I booked a flight for Saturday morning. We'll see what happens, I guess. Timmy is coming over tonight, so I probably won't get to spend much time with Adelaide. I don't know what I'm going to do with myself. I don't really feel like writing that much. I guess I could play Civilization. I've been neglecting that game for a while. It's pretty much the only game I really like. I thought I would be more than this (that's a lyric from a song that's playing, but I don't feel like looking to see who it's by). I'm such a fuck up. I hope I'm not being too annoying–just stating what's on my mind. At least this wine isn't too bad. It tastes better now than it did the other day. There's a verse in Proverbs that says something about giving wine to those in mental anguish. I think it could be said that I'm experiencing mental anguish.

Larkin sent me a video on Facebook of his boyfriend and his flaccid penis. He wants me to come get naked with them. Larkin is one of my favorite people, and his boyfriend is this super cute twink. I've had a threesome with them before. I really enjoyed spooning his boyfriend. That was nice. He's very petite, not that I don't like larger guys. I hooked up with a cub once at Short Mountain, and it wasn't bad. Speaking of which, my plan was to write about Short Mountain around the time I'd be going by Murfreesboro, but clearly that's not going to happen anymore. I think I've mentioned it before, but I don't remember what I said about it. This is a clusterfuck of a book. I'm sorry. Adelaide had to run an errand, but she should be back in an hour or so. I want to spend time with her because I am sad–at least until Timmy comes over, at least. I'm sure they're going to want to do it. There's some screamo song playing. I usually don't like this type of music, but right now I'm feeling it.

I took yet another shower because I was feeling gross. Nicole just messaged me and told me our friend is in jail. She got pulled over, and they found a pipe in her car. I'm assuming it was a meth pipe. She doesn't know that Nicole knows she does meth, but I kind of told Nicole. The last time I smoked meth was with her, actually. I'm such a shittie friend. I just have a problem keeping my mouth shut. Actually, I was trying to help them. Her friend was worried Nicole might judge her, and I kind of tested the waters to see if she would. She doesn't, though. She also pretty much already knew. I mean, you can usually tell if someone's on meth.

The last time I was staying with Adelaide, I was going through some shit and off my medicine. I remember one night I was in her room, and Timmy was there. They were cuddling, and I asked Timmy if he wanted to cuddle. I think it probably freaked him out, since he's so young and country. We've been fine this go round, though. I'm ready for her to be home, but she's probably going to go to sleep until Timmy gets off work and comes over late tonight. I have to pee.

Michael messaged me and mentioned us writing a song on Saturday. Hopefully that'll be cool. That's a good substitution for physical intimacy, I think. I need to be good, anyway. He's married, and I'm pretty certain he's completely heterosexual, anyway. I really wish I could be straight or a woman. I think it'd be easier to be a woman, though. I told him he'd basically become a main character in my book. He has no idea. I thought I would be more than this. That's a lyric from a song that's playing. I identify. It's a song called "Wasted Days" by Cloud Nothings. I've never heard of them, but I'm definitely feeling it. At least Spotify gets me. I need to trim my toenails. I'm going to do that now. I also need to take my weed candies out of the bag since I'm going to be flying. I don't think anyone will know what they are. I hope not, at least. That better not be foreshadowing. Maybe I should leave them here. I really wanted to bring back gifts for people, though. At least weed is decriminalized in Atlanta. I swear, I'm going to turn into a cigarette.

I told Michael he was basically becoming a main character in my book. He said he couldn't wait to read it. I told him I hope he won't judge me too harshly and that it's pretty damn raw. He said he likes raw. I hope he means that. I'm pretty sure he has no clue that I objectified him. He knows I think he's cute, though. But he's married. I don't want to be a homewrecker. He's straight, probably, anyway. I think I'm going to go play Adelaide's guitar for a while.

Well, I played for a bit and recorded myself singing one of my songs. I was going to upload it to Facebook, but I looked like shit, so I didn't. Plus the file size is entirely too big. I'm back in my room. Samson came up and licked me a bunch on the face while I scratched his back. The dog that doesn't like me came, too, oddly, but he wouldn't come up to me. I don't know why he's scared of me. Oh yeah, Adelaide told me he had an accidental encounter with Timmy's boot one time. Maybe that's why. I have to pee again.

Adelaide just got home. She's going to shave her legs and take a nap until Timmy gets here. I might do the same (minus the shaving the legs part).

Well, I ended up eating a couple pieces of weed chocolate, and I've been watching this series of trash gay movies called Eating Out. They make me feel like less of a pervert, I guess. I started thinking about Sodom, though. I don't know if I've mentioned this, but did you know that in Ezekiel it says that the sins of Sodom were pride, abundance of bread, and careless ease while they did not help the poor and needy. I feel like I suffer from sloth, gluttony, and sloth sometimes, but I do try to help the poor and needy whenever I have the chance. It also says they became haughty and did abominations. Am I haughty? I think I can definitely be haughty. And if spilling your seed is an abomination, I've definitely been abominable. I haven't had anal sex in a while, though. Does God hate me? Why the fuck was I made like this? I feel so unclean. Did King David feel this way about Jonathan? What did they mean when they said David exceeded? Doesn't that mean to grow larger? Or does it mean he cried more? Maybe it was both. I don't know. At least David was able to have children, though. That's one mitzvah I don't know if I'll ever complete. Fuck, I don't want to be wicked.

My stomach feels so empty, but I don't want to eat. I think I'll take another shower instead. That's weird, I was going to text my Jewish therapist, but I can't find our conversation on my phone. Anyway, I have to pee and then shower.

This beautiful song came on while I was in the shower. "The Big Idea" by Black Books. I don't know what they're saying, but it's beautiful. Black Books. I wish I were a black woman. Is that racist? I love black women. If I were to mate with a woman, I would want her to be black. Mixed babies are so cute, although from talking to a few I've learned that they sometimes get shit on worse than black or white people when it comes to racism. That sucks. Racism is stupid. I've just really admired most of the black women I've met for whatever reason. I've admired a lot of white women, Hispanic women, Jewish women, and... I don't think I've ever really gotten to know any asian women. Well, nevermind, there was Liza. But she was only just becoming a woman when I met her. I think she was 16 when I was 15. She may have been 15, though. We made out outside at our hotel. This old couple saw us and were thrilled. That's the only time that's happened to me in my life. That would never happen with an old couple unless they're gay maybe. Even then, a lot of old gay men are bitter, like me. Anyway, I also fingered her in the movie theater. But I never got an erection. She was pretty, too, and really cool. I don't understand myself.

Aimee Mann is playing now. I love her so much. I saw her at Music Midtown once. Her music really touches me in a comforting way. Cigarettes and Red Vines. I wish I had some Red Vines. I need to keep this gag from going too far, whatever this gag is. I know that's not what she probably intended for this song, but that's how I'm currently interpreting it, probably since

I'm high. Maybe I need to stop blaming myself. Maybe she's right.

That "Oh Mandy" song is playing again. I like this song. I like the sound. I miss Mandy. I need a tarot reading and an energy healing. Are those kosher? I'd be such a horrible Jew. I'm too meshuga. I think I'm going to incorporate that into my title or something. I don't want to come off anti-Semitic, even though I might be Semitic. Maybe the Muslims have it right. Does anyone really have it right? Did you know that Ashkenazi Jews have the highest IQ of any ethnic group? That says something. My former housemate in LA is Ashkenazi. She is wonderful. She is one of the best people I've ever known—so creative, just, and nice. I love her. Her mom makes good chicken soup, too. I miss her. She got my back once, which was awesome. I'll never forget that.

Wow, I just sent her a picture of what I said about her, and I realized she ignored me the last several messages I sent her. I forgot I had unfriended her. I feel weird now. My face is really hot. I want to cry. She's a mom now, though. So there's that. I'm just some crazy faggot. I'm having really bad thoughts now. This fucking song that is playing is super synchronic right now. Forrest Whitaker by Bad Books. I think I mentioned this before, but it's playing again. This is a bad book, isn't it? Fuck. I'm a shittie person and a shittie thinker and writer and everything. I'm just shittie. I want to cry.

I hate my body. I want to get rid of it. Maybe that would help my mind or soul or whatever. I don't know. I'm too much of a pussy to kill myself, though. I want to cry.

Maybe I should kill myself. For years when I would ask God what I should do with my life, I had a voice in my head that would tell me to kill myself. Chabad and Catholics both think suicide is the only unforgivable sin. I guess that makes logical sense. But in the New Testament Jesus says that the unforgivable sin is blasphemy of the Holy Spirit. What if he was just a sorcerer? The Egyptians were sorcerers, supposedly. Just because you can do magic doesn't mean you're a god. Who the fuck knows? I want to fucking cry goddamnit. I was so close. I was so close. I'm such a pathetic loser. I need a cigarette.

Won't someone please fucking come and save me? "We Begged 2 Explode" by Jeff Rosenstock. My eyes are actually watering a little bit. There it comes.

It didn't last long, though. At least my eyes are wet. That is oddly soothing. I feel like Spotify is stalking me. Maybe I'm a psychopath. I don't know. I don't know what the fuck is wrong with me. Maybe I was dropped on my head as a baby. Actually I was. My mom said someone flipped me over into the ditch and left me there when I was in my stroller. I think it was my sister or cousin or something. I don't know. My Facebook Messenger just dinged. I'm nervous.

My Ashkenazi friend just messaged me back. She said that's very sweet and asked me how everything is. I told her. I told her I was high and that writing brings out both good and bad emotions, which is True. I don't think I know what to do. I just forgot what I was thinking. I feel like someone or something is keeping me from either thinking or typing a certain thing. This is a weird feeling, but it happens sometimes.

I don't know. I know I say that a lot. But it's usually at least true, if not True. What about TRUE? I don't think I could handle TRUE. Fuck that. Major existential crisis. No fucking thank you. I'll pass on that. Nope. Nope. Nope. Get it out of my head. Maybe I should end this book. But this is only the beginning of the third part. Fuck. What do I do? What do I do? Is this art? Is this for a therapist? Shit. A rabbi? A priest? An imam? Random Southern Baptist Preachers names that I'm remembering but am too afraid to type. Fuck. Fuck. Fuck. I shouldn't say fuck. What do I do? Everyone gets to make one big mistake. That's what the current song is telling me. Define big. I've made countless mistakes, I think. I don't like this song. Next.

"The Only Living Boy in New York". I love this song. I especially identified with it when I lived in NYC, of course. Fuck, there are so many people who don't like me anymore. Like Yva. Yva was cool, but I'm pretty sure she hates me. I should talk to Krist Novoselic about this. He's losing his hair, too. I was never famous, though. I kind of don't want to be famous. I don't know. Veritas. Veritas. Veritas. Maybe some people aren't playable characters. That's a fucked up idea.

When I was a little kid I was going to make a newsletter called Veritas. I printed out the layout on my dot matrix printer. I never wrote any articles for it, though. I miss that computer. It was a 486sx/25 with 4 GB of Ram and a 210 MB hard drive. It also had a 2400 bps modem, which is how I ended up meeting Liza and Alix and Alli and everyone. But I also looked at a lot of gay porn. Oh, the first song I ever downloaded was a WAV file of The Wallflower's One Headlight. I actually ended up meeting the actual guy who wrote that song in Venice. He had just divorced from his wife, and she got half the house or something. But he made all his money from suing Jacob Dylan, I think. Oh, the rabbi whose class I was taking is friends with Jacob's father. Synchronicity. I don't know.

This song just told me that. Literally. The Halo Benders–something about Virginia. Hey, that's where I lost my virginity. See? It's happening. This happens sometimes. I'm not going to say I don't know because I do know that. Am I savage? Fuck I hope my family never reads this book. I wouldn't mind if my dad's sister read it, though. I wouldn't mind if his brother read it, but he's dead. But that's about it. Maybe my nephew–I don't know. That might be kind of weird. But he did tell me he loved me even though I was gay once. He's an accountant now. His wife is an accountant, and they've made me a great-uncle. I am proud of them. That kind of makes me want to cry.

Sonic Youth is playing now. "The Diamond Sea". I thought I was quantumly connected to a diamond once. That was one of my visions that came true. Oh yeah, I haven't mentioned my visions yet. Fuck. And Short Mountain. I need to talk about that, too. But it makes me really fucking nervous. I'm pretty sure that's the iceberg. I'm fucking terrified, though. I mean, I did fucking monologues about it in my play last year. Not many people came to see it, though. But still. My director thought it was interesting, at least, as did my cast mates, I think. Wait, I can write a book about writing a book about my life and the play about my life. Maybe this could be a play. Fuck that. Maybe. I don't know. Probably not. Damn you, Sonic Youth. A musical. Yeah, a musical. Fuck yes.

It sucks that you can't like, read my mind when I'm not typing. You miss a lot. Like, my mind just said, "Yes, you!", but I didn't type that until now. That happens quite often, so if this has come off a bit choppy, that's probably why. It's just a side effect of not being a perfect transcriber. I'm also too nervous to mention certain things, I guess. I wish I could make some good new friends through this. It would be nice to be able to be completely honest with someone without them disliking you. Yes, I just reminded myself of Yva. Everything Is connected.

Facebook is the devil. Or is it? It's extremely good and extremely bad. The internet in general is, I think. But is the extremely good worth the extremely bad? The Internet fucked me up. For real. For real, for real, for real. I guess it did, at least.

My Ashkenazi friend's name sounds a lot like the Queen of Heaven's name in Hebrew. I think it's the Queen of Heaven, at least. I don't know if that's the Moon or what. It probably is. She's the queen of the night, according to Genesis. The Catholics call Mary the Queen of Heaven. It's called Sin in some languages and Nanna in others. Nanna is what my nephew and niece call my mother. I thought she was the Moon for a while. Luna. Cynthia. Artemes. I met Artemis at Short Mountain. There's this gazeebo there with astrological symbols painted on the ceiling, and we had sex in the middle of it. She was in male form, apparently. Very woodsy creature. I don't think he brushed his teeth very often, but he was beautiful. I brush my teeth daily, but they're still fucked up.

I never understood why Artemis was associated with the moon, though. Are they all the same being? Are they even real? Maybe there's just one god. Did Abraham go through this? I met Neptune, too. He was really nice. I felt like he was my brother, since I'm quantumly connected to Jupiter. Possibly. I don't know.

Do I want to be a superhero or a crazy person? Is it even my choice? I really need to open up about what happened. I mean, what if my fears are correct? It makes me want to throw up. I just need to do it. I need to do it. I need to smoke a cigarette first. Fuck.

See, I felt protected, I guess, when I talked about this in the play at college. It was real life. They were real people. But you never know with the Internet. I mean, I know they're real people, but people on Reddit can be assholes. Trolls do fucked up things. Do I really want this shit out there? Am I a troll? I mean, am I a stereotypical old gay man who doesn't have a family, basically? I mean, I have a family, but I don't have a partner and a place and a dog and all that shit. I wish I were straight. I'd be Adelaide's partner, if she'd have me. But I'd want Timmy or someone to be there because I don't like vaginas. That's horrible. Gross. Shut up... damn, I almost typed my real name. Fuck.

Mona just messaged me on FB. Bear. That's his name now. Bear. I think. I'm assuming. That's horrible. I've got to change these names. I don't want anyone to read this anymore, except maybe a few people. Maybe Paul can write a movie inspired by this craziness. David Lynch could help. And his daughter. That would be kind of neat. I don't know if I'm interesting enough, though. I feel stupid now.

I'm going to take a shower.

"23" by Blonde Redhead is playing again. I had a lot of thoughts in the shower, most of which I have forgotten. I thought about mikvahs. They're like Jewish baptisms. I want to be spiritually clean like for real. Maybe I should lay off the weed and go back to school. I don't understand what I'm supposed to do with this apparent part I've been given. You have no idea what I'm talking about, do you?

I wish you could be inside my head. There's so much you just don't know. I wish our souls could dance in the dark. I wish that would remind you of Bjork, too. If that reminded you of Bjork, please be my friend. I'm going blind in my left eye. That triggers a flood of thoughts. If you were my friend, I'd tell you all about them. I even have a song about one of the things involving a fucked up eye. You can still be my friend even if you haven't seen that movie. I feel bad now. If you were my friend, I would also tell you why this song.. nevermind. If you've actually read this whole book and would like to be my friend, I would like to be your friend. I just hope that's not too many people. I mean, I hope people don't not want to be my friend, but I really don't want to be famous–not for this. I just don't want bad shit to happen to anyone including myself. That's why I need to change the names.

Dig deeper. I need to dig deeper. Iceberg. What iceberg? Which iceberg? I'm surrounded by icebergs. I need someone to read this and tell me what to do. I feel like my train has been derailing for days. Will Paul actually read it?

Bear is so cool. I don't know if he'd want to read this, though. I'm kind of embarrassed. He messages me really sweet things all the time. I don't know if he realizes I'm not nearly as attractive as I was when I met him. I really like him, but I'm not sure if my fucked up sex drive will get turned on by a vagina, unfortunately. Plus I think if I were with someone with a vagina I'd definitely want to have kids once I'm stable and fixed. He just said he'd take care of me if I went there. He just got an art grant or something. Maybe I should be a woman. But I'm losing my hair and I have fucked up teeth.

Maybe I need to stop trying to type everything I think. Is catfish kosher? I mean, why isn't catfish kosher? Stop it. Communicating is hard–well, communicating your intended meaning is hard. Brains suck. Fuck brains. I wish I were a goldfish. Fuck, I'm hearing the same songs over and over now. This is some bullshit. See, if I were a goldfish, I would have a shittie memory for shit like this. I feel nauseous.

This is futile. My whole body hurts. I'm going to take a bunch of Neurontin. All I have to drink up here is wine, though, and chasing pills with wine kind of sucks. But fuck it.

I actually had a swig of Mountain Dew left, so that was better than I thought it would be. Fuck, it's after 3 in the morning, and I'm still awake.

Some music by a black woman is playing, and it's kind of stressing me out. It's the beat, I think. I can't understand what she is saying, really. She's talking really fast. I guess that's one stereotypical young hood black (and country white boy) thing I don't like: the music. I mean, sometimes when I can understand the lyrics it's great, but it's really the style of music that I just don't like. It gives me anxiety. If that's racist, I'm sorry, but I don't know what to do about it.

I feel like such a waste of space. Adelaide said maybe I should adopt a new persona. Maybe I should be a woman. My body is starting to hurt a lot. I wish there was a reset button on life. I just want to start over. I'm delusional–no one is going to like this piece of shit. I'm going to take a shower.

I'm cold and wet, and my brain is pretty fried. I'm going to bed. Night.

CHAPTER XII

Wanda, my potential editor, hasn't responded to my email in three days. Maybe she is a villain. I don't know. I just know that people ignore me a lot. It's just something people like to do these days. A lot of people think I'm too crazy or something to respond to, I think. Whatever.

I took a shower and am listening to some pretty chill music. I need to brush my teeth and eat some cereal or something–not particularly in that order. I think I might play Adelaide's guitar for a while. She's at work for three more hours. Frosted Flakes first, though, definitely.

Ok, that was pretty tasty. I also took three Neurontin because I'm an addict, I guess. Maybe I won't eat anymore candy today. The rabbi says it alters your mind. Does it seem to do that to me? It probably does.

I have to confess something. I don't really want to play the guitar that much. I was hoping Timmy would be in her room, so I could talk to him, but he's gone. I'm so fucking co-dependent or something. I rely on people's company too much. I don't know why. Being around people, in general, usually makes me feel better.

Today is a week from Purim. This was supposed to be the last day I write, but things have changed. I haven't even told you some of the really crazy shit yet. I could think of a good reason for that if I wanted to, but I'm trying to be as truthful as possible, for the most part. It might be nothing, though. Maybe I'm just crazy. I'm going to lie down until these pills kick in.

I'm having extremely homicidal thoughts about this guy who works at the bus company. He won't refund my money because I used profanity yesterday on the phone. Miller Transportation is an evil company. Absolutely evil. I hate this planet.

I hate this book. This is so fucking stupid. Why am I even writing this? No one will probably ever read it. It's a huge fucking piece of shit. I want to die. I wish I could just go to sleep and not wake up. If I knew of a painless way to go, I'd do it in a heartbeat. I don't want to live anymore. I'm over it. It's one disappointment after another. It just gets worse and worse. What's the fucking point? Maybe I should slit my wrists. I don't want Adelaide or her dad to have to find my body, though. Finding someone dead is hard.

I'm on the phone with my mom. She is such a fucking cunt. Goddamn her. She told me to grow up and act like a man. This is the same bitch who pointed to her vagina and told me to get into it. This is the same bitch who has told me three times to "do what I want" when I told her I wanted to kill myself. Maybe I should fucking do it. I keep putting it off like a goddamn pussy bastard. I want to die. I want to fucking die. I hate this world. I hate people. I hate myself. I don't want to live anymore. I really, really fucking don't. My goddamn therapist won't even return my calls. Maybe my fucking plane will crash. Maybe someone will read this book and put me out of my misery in a humane way. I hope so. If I had a gun right now I'd do it myself.

I'm on hold with the receptionist at my mental health clinic. She is really nice. I can't stop crying. She told me I should go to the hospital, but I don't want to be hospitalized again. I don't want to be a man. I hate being me. I hate it so much. It's a fucking nightmare.

I want to have a husband and kids and a nice kitchen and a dog and a cat and a garden. I want to bake cookies. I want to learn how to sew.

Fuck it. I made an appointment with a therapist for Monday. I watched the rabbi a little with Adelaide, and he basically called me out for being a wicked, arrogant fool. I think that's pretty accurate. I don't know what to do other than die.

Paul emailed me back. I had told him I wanted to die because of this book. He said that I've survived so much tragedy and experienced so much joy, so it's worth continuing. Wanda also emailed me back. She didn't get my last message. I thought she was ignoring me. I feel bad for unfriending her on Facebook now.

I'm drinking the rest of my wine, and I ate some more weed chocolate. Fuck it. I feel like an abomination. Maybe I'll just embrace it. I don't know how to be a good person, at least according to God's supposed rules or whatever. I'm definitely not a mensch. I feel like this big ball of pain and sadness. The rabbi said that ill people only do negative things to feel better or something. That's definitely me. I'm so fucked up. Should I really just kill myself? I don't know. I feel like that's inevitable, though. Maybe this book can be my suicide note.

The therapist I spoke to kept asking me to tell her one good thing about myself. The only thing I could come up with, as usual, was that I am resilient.

Oh God, I'm looking at a picture of Josh and me. I miss him so much. I was so content and stable and comfortable with him. Why did he have to die? Do you know how fucked up it is to wake up and find someone you love dead? It's absolutely horrible. I've lost so many people, though–way more than most my age. I don't understand why. Is this part of God's plan or something? It kind of seems like a fucked up plan.

It's 4:52 in the afternoon. I think I'll take another shower.

It's 5:12. I keep fantasizing about killing those people at the bus company. Whatever. I think I'm going to jerk off. Sin is apparently the only thing that helps, apparently. I'm a wicked, arrogant fool.

Nevermind, I don't feel like it. It would take too much energy to try to get it up, and porn just isn't that interesting to me right now. I'll just finish this bottle of wine and whine some more.

I'm looking at my painted nail and daydreaming about being a girl. That would be nice. I think that would fix all my problems. Unfortunately, I have male pattern baldness, and I don't really want to wear a wig. I'd be an ugly girl, probably. Ugly people have it hard. Beautiful people can definitely have it hard, too, though. Life can be shittie. I actually think being beautiful when you're young and living a long time is a terrible experience. That's how I feel about myself, at least. I used to be so cute. Some people have told me I look the best I've ever looked now, but they might just be trying to make me feel better. I don't agree. Well, I'm pretty popular at leather bear bars and shit. People there are generally pretty nice. Maybe I should find one in Georgia. I think there's one or two in Atlanta. I really need to get my teeth fixed first, though. The director of my play's little nephew or whatever pointed out that I was missing a tooth. That's why I never smile.

This one guy told me he thought my broken tooth was cool. That's pretty weird. I think it's pretty gross. I wish I were black. Did you know that black people have like three times more enamel on their teeth than white people? They have much better genetics–probably because the rest of us mutated when we left Africa or the Middle East or wherever humanity began–probably Africa. Theologians might disagree.

White people are also crazier than black people, I think. Have you ever heard of a black serial killer? I haven't? I know I'm crazy as fuck, though. Anyway, sorry if that's racist.I either want to be a black woman or a white redhead. Sometimes when I'm in the shower I imagine myself as a beautiful redheaded woman. I actually have the red hair gene. My hair was bright red when I was little, but now it's brown. I have some red in my beard, though.

Goddamn, I need to tell you a story. This is a memoir, for fuck's sake. Ok, I guess I could tell you about my visions.

In 2015, I started having these visions. I was on Adderall at the time, so I don't know if that had something to do with it. But I had a vision that Bill Gates was trying to build a type of Zion near my hometown. I thought it had something to do with the Masons. I also had a vision that I was quantumly connected to a diamond star.

The next year, my mom's cousin told us that her son was a contractor and had been working on 4,000 acres of land that Bill Gates bought in our county to be his "bug out spot".

Then I was at a friend's house (the one who gave my flame tattoo), and this guy came over. I'm pretty sure he was on drugs, but he pulled out his tablet computer from his bag, and it had the Order of the Eastern Star logo as the wallpaper. I told him that my grandma was Worthy Matron, and he took me to a back room. He pulled out a dollar bill and pointed to the all-seeing eye. He said something about "Father, Son, Holy Ghost. Heaven, Hell, and Earth". He told me I was a star and that there were other stars in Warner Robins. He told me my parents must've paid a high price for me. Then he gave me a skeleton key, and attached to it was a key chain with a diamond star on it, just like my vision. I asked him if they were nefarious, and he said he only knew that they would make bad things happen to get you to come back home because they love you. Well, that has definitely happened to me a tremendous amount of times.

August 14, 2016 I came home from the same house and laid down. I wasn't tired because I had taken an Adipex (diet pill). I closed my eyes, and I saw the end of the world. I don't know what I saw–I was just left with the feeling. When I opened my eyes, hovering above my bed were two metallic rings that were intertwined. I had never seen anything like it before. I've never had a visual hallucination before, either. I was in shock. I bolted downstairs and knocked on my mom's door. I couldn't even speak. I ended up sleeping with her that night because I was so in shock.

The next day, I went on YouTube, and the first recommended video was about the New World Order. In it, it showed exactly what I saw–supposedly the "wheel within the wheel" that Ezekiel saw in his vision.

I Googled that date to see if anyone else had experienced anything weird. I found where someone had put a cube in the Georgia Guidestones that had the numbers "8, 14, 20, 16" engraved on it–the date that I saw the wheel within the wheel. That was also Tish B'av–the same day that is the messiah's metaphorical birthday according to the Jewish sages.

I really thought I was the reincarnation of David, you know. And I found out the interior of Jupiter might be a giant diamond because it rains hydrocarbons. And Jupiter is called the "King David planet".

I know this sounds fucking crazy, but I'm telling you the Truth. I know I would be a fucked up messiah, but I know how to achieve peace in the Middle East. Muhammad made treaties with certain sects of Jews and the Smaritans, the supposed "keepers of the Law". If people in Israel could follow the Torah by following the ways of others, perhaps, there could be peace. I don't know. I know it's probably delusions of grandeur, but still. The Chabad website talks about the dangers faced by David regarding reincarnation. That was one of the main reasons I wanted to convert. I want to perform tikkun on my soul. I need to. It feels so dirty or something–so lost, so broken. Oh, my birthday is Hitler's birthday, but it was also Yom Hashoah that day (Holocaust Memorial Day). And the number of my full name in Hebrew has the gematria numerical value of 541. That's the same value of the word Israel and also the tenth Star of David number. The number ten corresponds to the letter yod, which originally was the symbol of an arm–like the arm of God. My mother's maiden name is also Young, and Christians say Jesus was born of a virgin according to prophecy. The word they translate to "virgin" is actually alma, which means "young woman.". And my mom is literally a Young woman.

Anyway, this is getting too crazy, I know. You think I'm insane. Maybe I am.

So I just got off the phone with my good friend Nicole. I love her so much. She's been my best friend when I'm in Georgia (Adelaide is my best friend here) along with Greer. Nicole has an autistic fifteen year old and little boy. I love them all.

One day at school, Nicole's daughter mentioned a dream she had about being chased by a plushy octopus. She said I was in the dream (by the way, she is very autistic and it's difficult to communicate with her sometimes). Well, the teacher told the principal who told someone who told DFCS or something that they were concerned she was being molested by me.

They investigated for a while, and I wasn't allowed to go over to Nicole's house. When the cops found out it was me, they didn't believe it, since they know I am extremely gay. Plus I wouldn't mess with a fifteen year old autistic kid anyway. That's messed up. I told my sister about it, and she was so pissed off. She called the teacher, but the teacher said it wasn't her fault. Still, that's fucked up to be accused of something like that. Oh, when the cops interviewed her daughter, they asked her if I had ever touched her and where. She said I touched her tummy, which isn't true, but whatever. Anyway, that's when they found out that nothing happened.

Oh, Nicole sometimes gives me pain pills when I'm feeling really bad. But then she runs out before she can get a refill, and that sucks. She is extremely generous, though. I try to make up for it by going to the store for her and doing her dishes, but I feel like I should be doing more. She really needs all the help she needs since she also suffers from physical and mental maladies. She's a really good person, though.

I'm excited to see her and also Michael tomorrow. I think I realized that the best thing I like about Michael is that he likes me. He makes me feel like a better person, even if I'm not really.

Shit, I posted on Facebook for people to tell me a good memory they had of me, and I am crying like a baby.

I think I used to be a good person, kind of. I may have had ulterior motives at some points, though.

Okay, I just cried for a really long time. I can barely see the screen. My nose is stopped up. I still can't stop. It breaks my heart.

Oh shit, I just realized the light wasn't on the screen. That's why I couldn't see. Much better.

Fuck. I wish Adelaide would wake up. The therapist I talked to earlier said that people won't like you if you don't like yourself. I don't know if that is true. I hate myself. Does that mean everyone hates me?

Most of my memories are bad. That's just how it is. It sucks, but it is what it fucking is. I hate that phrase. Whatever. I'm sad and high. This song "Sister" by Angel Olsen is really nice. I haven't paid attention to what she's saying. I am now, though, and I concur.

Samson just came in the room and licked my hand. He gets really excited when I pet him–a little too excited, really. He left. Now the cat is leaving. Well, fuck. Oh well. Hey, he's back. Nope, he's gone. I think he might want to go out, but I don't feel like getting up.

So, I ended up hanging out with Adelaide and watching Fiddler on the Roof, kind of. We talked about a lot of stuff. It's really cold in this room, but I'm stalling because I don't know if I should mention it or not. Oh shit, I need to text her my flight time. Seven in the morning. I'm going to have to get up right after I fall asleep. Maybe I can nap on the plane.

Ha, my friend Dixie just reminded me of the time we went to the Twisted Anchor in St. Mary's and got shit faced. We kept calling it the Twisted Ankle. And I remember I almost got naked for a pool bet or something. I was in my boxers for a while. That was a fun night.

See I'm kind of anxious about mentioning some people, like one of my old co-workers from The Base. The one I'm thinking about who commented on my Facebook post about memories is a lovely woman I used to chat with at the smoking gazebo. But I think she's too wholesome to read this book, so I'm not going to mention her name so I won't have to tell her she's in it. Actually I loved all the ladies and couple gentlemen that would frequent the gazebo.

Sorry, my mind was going to the idea that I'll ever even have this published. Who would want to read this, anyway? It's pretty terrible probably. Damn, my stomach is full of ice cream cake. I almost feel like I need to purge. I have two cigarettes left. It's 8:19 at night. I have to get up at 5 or something. I should attempt to sleep soon, maybe.

I feel like the current song that's playing is hugging me. It's "Waving, Smiling" by Angel Olsen. I've never heard this before, but it is absolutely beautiful.

Adelaide texted back. We leave at 5:30. I need to set my alarm for 5:00. That'll give me time to get my shit together and take a shower and everything.

I'm about to fall asleep. Goodnight.

CHAPTER XIII

I'm watching The Magicians Panel at Comic-Con 2019. Hale likes Kate Bush. That makes me happy. Is Kate Bush still in hiding? Has anyone heard from her in a while? I would like to have tea with Kate and Hale. I'm high, by the way. It's 2:28 in the morning. I feel pretty good, though.

Fuck, I need a cigarette. This vape is just not doing it. Okay, I got a pack of Adelaide's dad's Montclair Blacks. They're a bit bitter, but it's a cigarette. Some people like bitterness. Plus I'm used to smoking menthols, so all non-menthols would probably seem bitter to me. They really need a cigarette rehab. Why the fuck does this not exist? I've never got a sign that I shouldn't do heroin, but I've definitely gotten signs that I shouldn't smoke cigarettes.

There's a line in one of my songs that talks about all the stories that I won't tell. Fuck, I was compelled to sing it, but my ukulele is in my suitcase downstairs.

My mind is racing with stories that I haven't told–like the time this guy lured me into the bushes in Hollywood to smoke meth, but he took a knife out and made me show him my dick. And the time I stole $400 from my granddad's car when he was dying in the hospital because I thought I could make it back plus some if I played the lottery. I was going to put it back, but I lost. I don't know why my brain so rarely goes to good memories. It's usually bad stuff. Maybe I'm a negative person. Are all people with negative blood types negative people? I have wondered that before. I'm not trying to add to any conspiracy theories, though. People are people and need love regardless of genetics. That's easier said than done, though. They found my blood type on the shroud of Turin, but I don't know what the Rhesus value was.

I'm so ready for my yDNA test to come in so I can work on my genealogy some more. The highest concentration of my modal haplogroup is in Bosnia. I think like half the people have it. It's pretty rare in the rest of the world, though. There are a lot in Sardinia, too, for some reason. My haplogroup is hypothesized to have originated in the Middle East. Wait, no, that's my modal haplogroup–haplogroup I. Haplogroup I2, which I am a part of, has its highest concentration in Bosnia. Haplogroup I1, a genetic cousin, is found in high concentrations in Sweden and Finland. Our cousin, haplogroup J, is found mostly in the Middle East and the Mediterranean region. That's where you can find the Cohen modal haplogroup, which traces the supposed line of Aaron, I believe. Look it up yourselves. It could be the tribe of Levi. I always forget the genealogy.

Cohen Modal Haplotype–not haplogroup. There's a difference, but this isn't a book about genomics. Anyway, most white people are Haplogroup R, which is a cousin of my haplogroup and the Jews and Arabs, but we're very distantly related. They would be considered Asian, really, since they originated on the steppes. I think most Royal Europeans have been Haplogroup R. I don't think there has ever been European royalty with my haplogroup. Bill Gates has it, though. So did Davy Crockett and Elvis and a few other famous people. I've wondered if yDNA-linked chromosomes may affect personality or something. It's possible. There have been Chinese studies that concur.

I feel like this knowledge could lead to an entire new genre of discrimination. What would you call it though? Geneticist is already a word. That's kind of funny. Wait, would that make "racist" mean someone who studies race? That would definitely make me racist then. I was compelled to share this on Facebook, but I think I chickened out.

I do that a lot. I either overshare or undershare. I guess I'm an extremist. If I were religious, I'd probably end up being an extremist. The rabbi says that you should always take the moderate path, though–lean neither to the left nor to the right.

I feel like I'm being a talebearer, which is a negative commandment in the Torah. It says not to go running up and down the town telling tales or something. I don't remember the exact wording, and I'm too high to look it up. Should I be Jewish? I doubt any rabbi would have me if they read this tome. Can I even call it a tome? That sounds so pretentious, although I do say it to be funny or something sometimes.

My battery is low. I forgot what I was thinking about. Fuck. I'm having negative vibes now. That sucks. I want a shower, but my towels are wet. There are dry ones downstairs, but I don't feel like going downstairs. By the way, when I took a shower earlier, I counted nine cigarette butts that I left in there. That means I've taken nine showers since I missed the bus. Damn. On a side but related note, I wish I had less hair on my body and more on my head so I could dress like a girl and see what I'd look like. I've had several people tell me I should. But I feel like I'd look like a booger drag queen. No offense to booger drag queens. You guys are super funny. It makes you sexy in a weird way. I won't mention any names.

Jesus said that you defile yourself with what comes out of your mouth and not what goes into your body. Do fingers count? They probably do. I don't know. What would Jesus think? The only Jesus I know is a Mexican. He used to be one of my best friends. I've had so many good times with him. But when I went crazy he basically stopped talking to me. He also named his bands names that talk about being queer and schizophrenic, and I don't think they know any queer schizophrenics other than me. So I got upset because I felt like he was making fun of me the whole time, and after he ignored me when I wanted to hang out, I told him I was going to start a band called "asshole spic and his cunt of a wife" or something like that. I just thought of the meanest thing I could think of. I wish we were friends again, though. I'm still friends with his brother, who I thought was God for a while. I wish I hadn't gone crazy. It really fucked up my life. I need music.

I miss Jesus. I miss his parties. I miss everybody. It makes me want to cry. Fuck it. I'm over it. People change. Shit changes. I need to grow the fuck up, so they say. I'm 38 goddamn years old.

Do I want to be Wikipedia famous? I mean, you know, like people won't generally recognize me, but strangers will write about me on Wikipedia. That would be cool, as long it's not too bad or anything. No, I don't want to be famous for this book. Well, if I do, at least, I just don't want anyone to try to hurt me or anyone I've mentioned. That's all. If people get pissed, then they get pissed. Maybe then they'll talk about why they're pissed. We can open up a public dialogue about it or something. I'm just tired of fucked up shit.

So yesterday Adelaide and I were in the kitchen and talked for a long time about Bird. Bird was Adelaide's boyfriend. He was so beautiful and good to me. Once he came over to look for Adelaide, and I took him to my secret spot in the woods in the old limesink by the creek. We sat on either side of the creek, and the sunbeams hit his face, and it made him look like an angel. I was just staring at him in awe with my mouth open for a long time. He was so beautiful and looked so innocent. I think he has a very innocent but hurt soul. Well, had. I hope it's healed by now. I know it has been.

I was the last person to hang out with Bird. When I saw him, he was acting kind of crazy but was being nice to the cat. He had been thinking that worms were coming out of his body. He would save them in jars, but I'm pretty sure it was just skin or something. He also thought people were poisoning his water supply. I thought it was the meth, and I told him he should lay off of it, but he didn't agree. Adelaide and I agreed that it was probably more of the lack of sleep and food that did it.

Anyway, three days after I saw him, my mom tells me that she hears that Bird was shot. Fuck this makes me cry. Apparently he got into it with his mom, and his mom called 911. The police came, and Bird was at his shop holding his shotgun. He wouldn't put it down. He had told me no one was going to take him alive, and he was right. They put a bullet through his chest. He was alive for a while, but they didn't even try to help him. I couldn't get myself to watch the video.

I've lost so many friends. I could tell you so many stories about them. I don't know if I should, at least right now. It feels good to cry, but it's really hard bringing them up while I'm writing for some reason. I don't know why. I feel like it's easier for me to talk about it. It's weird. Or maybe I'm too lazy and there are so many people. That's probably it, in actuality. Shit. There was Lindsey, Heather, Joey, Landon, Randall (of course), Josh (of course), Justin, Jan, Billy, Dusty, Kameron, Antone (aw, Antone), and others probably who I have amazing memories with but are now gone. Nicolas. And Nicolas. He was so beautiful and sweet and crazy. I can't forget him. So many memories. It's pretty daunting to have to write about them all, though. I don't know why.

I think Greer just texted me accidentally. I haven't heard from a while, even though she's one of my best friends. I'll probably see her when I go back to Georgia, though. My flight leaves in a few hours. It's 3:42, and we're leaving at 5:30. I need to pack soon and take my tenth shower. That's a good even number. What am I going to wear, though? I have no idea what the weather is like in Atlanta. I'm assuming it's warmer than here. I'll probably just wear one of the plaid shirts Adelaide gave me. She is so good to me.

Aw, Greer just texted me that she wanted to check on me and that she missed me. That's really sweet. I'm surprised she is being sweet. She also sent me a picture of a watermelon. I would love some watermelon with a little bit of salt. That would be perfect right now. Damn. Anyway, Greer is about to call me I think.

She wants me to change her name to Jett Black, so I have to remember that when I edit–or somebody edits. That's going to be a lot of work to change the names. I still need to find out if I need to change celebrities' names. I really don't know if anyone will ever read this, anyway. Jett wants me to bring her back a weed candy because she's having dental issues, but I'm really nervous about flying with it now. I don't know. Okay, I need to find some clothes to wear.

Okay, Timmy's on his way to pick us up and take me to the airport. I'll write more later.

I'm on the way to the airport. I'm high. I didn't bring the rest of the candy with me, though. I'm kind of paranoid about flying, but I don't want to talk about it. I feel a little nauseous. My ears are cold because their windows are open. I'm in the back seat of Timmy's 2021 Mustang that he's super proud of. He just made a corny joke about me dying in an airplane crash. He said to get naked so'll they'll ask, "What the fuck happened to this dude?" I asked him what I should do if it doesn't actually crash and I'm naked. Adelaide said I'd be naked and in handcuffs.

It is what it is. I'd really rather die peacefully in my sleep. I feel like my existence is too big, and I need to live more. L'Chaim. I need a drink. I want to be a Jew. I really need structure in my life. I want to be humble. I also like the holy days. I was looking into the Karaite Jews, but there aren't too many of them around, I don't think. They interpret the Torah the way they want, supposedly. I don't know, though. Most Jews these days think the rabbinic texts including the Oral Law are crucial, even though I've been told infallibility is a Christian concept. I just don't know. I really don't. I wish I knew. That would be amazing.

Timmy just made a really weird noise that sounded like a goose or something. I'm really high. I have no idea what's going on. Country music is playing, but I don't know what they're saying. He said it was called Dark Country or some shit. I'm really nauseous. I just had this long conversation with Adelaide, and

I have no idea what we were talking about. It's really fucking hot in this huge coat, but we're like 15 minutes away. Fuck it, I'm taking it off. Oh, we were talking about body dysmorphic disorder. Okay, trying to type is making me want to puke.

Okay, I'm waiting to board the plane. I fucking left my phone in Timmy's car, though. I don't know if that's a good thing or a bad thing. I hate wearing masks. I feel like I'm suffocating. I hate flying, even though it's the quickest way usually.

Now I'm on the plane. I think I'll try getting Michael's number from my laptop when I get my baggage. Maybe this is the only bad thing that will happen today. I can deal with that. Anyway, I'm going to try to take a nap before we get there. It's cold, and I want to snuggle under my coat.

Well, I guess the Michael thing is off. I couldn't get an Internet connection on my laptop, and there are no phones in the airport, so I just got on the shuttle and went back to Warner Robins. This nice black gentleman let me use his phone to call my mom, so that's cool. Sometimes black men are kind of homophobic around here more so than white people for some reason, so it's hit or miss how someone will react to me.

I'm not too upset about not being able to hang out with Michael. I kind of had a feeling the hands of fate would pull some strings. It's whatever. I told my mom to give Adelaide my pin number for my phone and tell her to call Michael to let him know what happened. I kind of regret leaving my weed candies behind. The guy on my shuttle said he travels with them all the time. Oh well. I'm really tired.

All these cars were stopped on the Interstate for a little dog with a pink color that was running around on the road. He almost got hit, but he made it across the road. I think he might be going back to the trailer park across the way. I can't wait to get to Macon and smoke a cigarette. Maybe they'll give me a few minutes to have a few puffs, at least.

I'm back at my parents' house. I took a nap, woke up, and went to Nicole's. She didn't have enough pain pills to give me one, so I bought some Kratom. I feel extremely suicidal. And I'm cold. It's cold outside and cold in my room. I can't get comfortable. I feel weighed down.

There's not much desire to write anymore. I don't even have the desire to masturbate or take a shower or smoke a cigarette. I just want to sleep forever. I want to be put out of my misery. I'd do it myself if I knew how. I wish there were just a pill I could take to fall asleep and not wake up. My dad has a gun in his room. I wonder if it's loaded. I'm just tired. I want this feeling to go away. There's no such thing as a good god.

Well, I laid down for a bit. The Kratom kicked in and helped some. I also took a shower. I'm considering going back to rehab. I messaged Daniel to see if he wanted to go, too, but I think he might be banned from there for being too crazy. I definitely need help, though. I just don't want to feel isolated there if there's no one to connect with. I also don't want to go overboard and develop a crush on another straight guy. I wish I could go to a rehab with just females. That would be ideal. Anyway, Medicare won't pay for treatment if all you do is use marijuana. I'm not sure if Suboxone counts. I guess I could find someone to give me some meth or a pain pill so I can piss dirty. I miss being able to smoke inside. This sucks. I'm also ready to end this book, even though I haven't hit the 60k word mark yet. There are things I haven't told you about, but I don't know if I have the energy. I took three more Neurontin and am debating on taking some more Kratom. I don't want to go get it out of the car, though. It's cold. The cold here is different because of all the humidity, I think. I want to get off, but I don't want to think about sex. I just want the endorphins. Fuck it, I'm going to the car.

Alright, it's been a while, and I'm feeling a little better. I talked to Jett. She's having really bad tooth pain on top of her normal physical and emotional pain, so I'm going to buy some Delta 8 THC at the vape shop tomorrow for us, I think. We can't afford to get a pain pill. It's $40 for one 30 mg oxycodone now. Ridiculous.

I'd be fine with half of one, but she needs at least a whole one.

I'm watching the cast of The Magicians chat on YouTube again. I envy gay men like Hale who seem to have their shit together. I assume he's gay, anyway. It must be nice. I'm just a fucking mess. I probably need to be euthanized.

It's been a long, shittie day. I think I'm going to try to pass out now.

CHAPTER XIV

When I woke up I thought it was like 8 in the morning, and I was pissed for waking up so early, but it was actually 4 in the afternoon. I called the vape shop, and they were closed, but they met me there so I could buy some Delta 8 THC gummies. I came over to Nicoles and gave Jett two green ones because that's the color she wanted. I ate two, too. We're waiting for them to kick in. I wasn't really sure how much we should eat. Jett said I was being rude for writing while we're hanging out, so I'm going to take a break.

Okay, Jett and I are high. I ate three, and she had sex. We're taking turns listening to songs on YouTube. She chose the Schitt's Creek version of "You're Simply the Best". I think I'm going to play Iron and Wine's "American Mouth". I didn't realize it was on Twilight—Nicole and Jett just informed me. Jett said the actress was really good as Joan Jett in The Runaways. I don't feel like typing anymore. I'm just going to chill and listen to music.

Blackee and Jaquellin are playing with a straw. Cowboy is loafing by a box. I love kitties. Nicole is about to go pick up her kid from the Dudley exit. He and his dad went on vacation in Tennessee. Jett doesn't want me to type because she'll be bored.

Jett is listening to IC3PEAK. I bought her a poster of theirs for Christmas. She's obsessed with Russia for some reason. They sound really good, though. I dig it.

Before this she was listening to "Wild World'. It reminds me of Skins. I miss that show—the first season of it, at least. Jett and I were obsessed with it. She skipped me, so it's my turn. I chose "Shadow of the Cross" by Sufjan Stevens. I love this song. It makes me want heroin, though.

Jett is playing "The Good Side" by Troye Sivan. She said she doesn't really like his music, but she likes this song. She says he's gay, but that's not why she doesn't like his music.

Our mutual friend Eve just came over. She has to get home before the sun goes down because she just got out of jail because she had four warnings for a busted headlight. We're going over there to smoke a little meth because her parents aren't there. We don't want to meet her boyfriend, though. We just want to get out of this THC high or whatever. We're just going to smoke a little bit and hang out for a minute. She said to give her ten minutes so she can go by the store first to get food for the kids.

Jett and I just danced horribly to "Now My Favorite Color is Blue" by K. Flay and Robert DeLong. We both really like this song. Jett is peeing, and then we're going to Eve's.

I'm back at my house. It's sometime after 10. I'm listening to Courtney Love on Spotify. "Hold On To Me". I think this might be the album Linda helped her on. Linda is Clementine's ex. We used to be Facebook friends, but I don't know what happened. I used to like listening to her sing karaoke songs. She was really famous in the 90s for her song "What's Up". I really like "Spaceman". Now I think she mostly helps write other famous peoples' songs like Pink and Christina Aguilera, if I'm not mistaken.

I want to take a shower, but I got spoiled being able to smoke while I shower in Indiana. I'm also kind of hungry, but I don't feel like eating. Sucks.

Cursive is playing. I saw them live once with Lori #1, I think. I really like this song–"From the Hips". Fuck I forgot to put on deodorant earlier, and I just smelled myself. It's not that bad, though. Smells like a freshly mown law. I really need to tell you the story about what happened tonight, but it's kind of long. I really like this song. I also really want a shower.

Alright, I'm out of the shower. I forgot to use the charcoal soap I got from Birchbox. Oh well. I used some other body wash, and it was good. I think the last box had a body wash called Bird in it. It reminded me of Bird. Speaking of which, Adelaide just messaged me to check on me. That was sweet. Also Nicole was mad we left because she wanted to try some gummies. I told her I'd bring her some tomorrow.

My mom called me upstairs to talk before I took a shower. She was crying and told me she took a Xanax because she was stressing out about me possibly doing meth like I did last time when I was crazy. I had stopped taking my meds, too, so that had a lot to do with it. Plus I snorted it instead of smoked it, which makes a big difference. If I have a little bump, I can't sleep for three days and go insane. If I smoke it, I'm fine. I smoked it tonight, of course. That's the only way Eve does it, I think. Man, she orders so many drugs from the Dark Web. That shit makes me paranoid. Fuck that. The Dark Web is evil as hell. I wouldn't mind trying some ketamine therapy for my depression, though. I'm thinking about doing it.

Eve told me the story tonight about how her ex broke into her house, tied her up, and raped her. He was the superintendent's son, I think. My dad knew he was in prison, but he didn't know about that. It happened in the house right next door to mine. My friend Landon used to live there (he died) because his mom had traded houses with Eve's parents after that happened.

So let me tell you about what happened tonight. My battery is low, by the way, so I'll try to make it short. Anyway, Eve said her parents would be gone until Sunday, but apparently none of us realized it was Sunday. Well, Jett thought she remembered her saying Monday, but anyway. We were smoking meth in her parents' room when her boyfriend yelled at us that they had just got home. We panicked. We bolted out of the room and started playing piano in the living room just in time. I told her dad I had come over to play piano. He believed me. I have never met her parents before, but I knew of her dad because he's been a professor at the college for like 40 years or something.

I ended up chatting with her parents for a long time. They are both really cool. I talked about history a lot with her dad, and I found out her mom and I are distant cousins through both my parents' sides (they're fourth cousins). We're all interbred here. I told her mom I was going to be changing the names of everyone in my book, but I didn't know if I should change celebrities' names. We talked about Cybil Shepherd for a while, not that I have much juicy gossip. She said she wanted to read my book, but I told her it's very adult. I think I would feel weird having her read it, although she told me she thinks Eve should write a book.

I feel like I haven't written very much today, but I've had a pretty good day. I really need to take my medicine tonight. I keep forgetting. Maybe I should go back to rehab. I don't know--I have a couple months to kill. I just don't want my mom to get pissed if she finds out I've been on something. I don't know. I don't know what I should do. I don't know who to ask, either. Oh, that's right, I talk to my therapist tomorrow at 1. I don't have a phone to set an alarm on, though. I really need to talk to her. She'll give me some good advice.

Modest Mouse is playing now. My old roommate Yva toured with them or knew them or something. She really liked their name. I like them a lot. They have a lot of good stuff, but this is "Missed the Boat". I dig it. I really want a cigarette. I really wish I could smoke inside–it's so cold out there.

I have a million ideas floating around my head. Did I miss the boat? What boat did I miss? I'll take a spaceship. Oh yeah, Eve's mom and I talked about Dr. Robert's wife. We're both distant cousins with her, too. This isn't public knowledge, but Dr. Roberts used to work at Area 51. I definitely need to change these names. Anyway, his step-son told me that. The only time I've ever brought him up to her, sne changed the subject to her chickens. I know she misses him a lot. He was a good man.

Sometimes I wonder if some of us here were part of some government experiment. Maybe it even had something to do with aliens. I don't know. It's just a hypothesis, I guess. Sometimes I don't know the difference between a hypothesis and a theory. Maybe it's just an idea. I mean, Jessica did say that he said he was working on something "bigger than the Internet". What the hell does that even mean? What could be bigger than the Internet except maybe uploading your consciousness or communicating with extraterrestrials or something. Oh, I read somewhere that there is supposedly this record of everyone's genealogy somewhere–like their actual genealogy. I don't know if that's true, but I would love to have access to that database if it existed.

I traced my maternal genealogy back to the gods of Northern Europe through my possible grandmother who married Harold Bluetooth. It's weird that we might share the same mitochondrial DNA. Supposedly it traces all the way back to the supposed gods that are buried in mounds in some small town in Sweden or something. I'm not sure about my dad's side, but for a while I thought they might be Jewish. There are people in Israel with my last name, but I guess that doesn't mean that much. I think my last name was originally French. My yDNA haplogroup is Semitic though, if you correlate the known haplotree with the Table of Nations according to the Bible. Some say I descended from Shem's son Lud. I don't know. They would be the Luddites, and I identify with the modern definition of that word sometimes–especially when it comes to the Internet. Or were they called the Luddim? Maybe both–I don't know. For a while I also thought I descended from David through his step-father the King of Ammon, who I thought might've been his biological father. I mean, it does say that he was different from the other sons of Jesse. And why did Jesse call him out? Maybe it's because he wasn't his biological son. David's potential father's real name in Hebrew means serpent. They say that people with the serpent bloodline have red hair. I have the red hair gene.

I don't know, though. Who knows what's true or not, really? I've wondered if I were actually a Nephilim. The Bible describes David as "ruddy", which some say means he had red hair. It also says that about Jacob's brother Esau. Prince Harry has red hair. I thought about Pierre, I think that is what her alias is, when I was in the shower. She went to school with Harry's wife. I miss her. I want to go dancing at Akbar. That would be fun. Am I too old to go out dancing now? I don't know. I want a cigarette. Why does it have to be so cold? I miss living in a Mediterranean climate. One of my therapists suggested that I move to Tel Aviv.

I feel bad for the Tel Aviv people, since it's mentioned in the Book of Revelation that the Tribe of Dan won't make up the 144,000. I don't know about that story, though. I have so many questions. Jett told me tonight not to talk about religion with Eve's father. I talk about religion way too much, and sometimes it annoys people or freaks them out or something. I don't know. I'm used to it.

My back hurts. I wish I had something for pain. Oh yeah, I could take some Neurontin. I forgot I had some. I hope there's some drinks in the downstairs refrigerator.

Okay, I got one of my mom's diet Cokes because I didn't want to go outside, even though Eve bought me a 12-pack of cokes at the store when she had to get peppermints. She's addicted to peppermints.

I hope these pills kick in soon. My back hurts like a motherfucker. Ugh, Diet Coke burps taste weird. I don't know if I'm going through withdrawals or what, but I physically feel like absolutely shit. Maybe I should go to rehab. I would definitely go if I could get someone I know to go with me, but Daniel is banned, and I don't know any other guys with Medicare that would go.

Oh, Jett was in a really bad car wreck when she was little, and it fucked up her brain. I feel like I should mention that since I talked about the Eve rape thing. She was also molested by her cousin, but I don't know if she'd want me to mention that. She just doesn't want her mom to read this. I don't want her mom to read this either, even though I love her mom, and her mom loves to read. She's a genius. She's had cancer for years, though, and the meds fuck up her memory now I think. Jett's dad died when we were young. That was a really sad funeral. He was a good man. He always used to say that I had a little sugar in my tank. I do.

Well, I took another shower and took my meds. I really don't want to masturbate, but I don't know how else to relieve this pain, so that's what I'm going to do. Fuck it.

Okay, I just got off to some old man fuck a twink. Good for him. It's whatever. I was just looking for the endorphins. It made me feel slightly better. I'm still hungry. Daniel told me he'd go with me to rehab, but then he remembered he only has 17 days left on his insurance. Plus he just moved in with a new guy after he broke up with his girlfriend. The cops saw her beating the shit out of him, and he still got a domestic violence charge. That sucks. I can't remember if I asked him if I could use his real name.

Your ship may be coming in. You're weak but not giving in to the cries and the wails of the valley below. That's from "A Better Son/Daughter" by Rilo Kiley that I am currently listening to. I want to be a better son or daughter. My dad would definitely prefer a son, although my sister thought I wanted to get a sex change at one point. She thought that's why I was crazy. Maybe it has something to do with it–I don't really know.

I need to pee. I also think I'm going to take an actual hot bath. That might be better. I don't feel like being in pain anymore.

Alright, that was an amazing bath. I was completely pain-free for so long. I had to get out because the water was turning cold, though. It was amazing. I was reminded of the time at Short Mountain when some woman kept putting wood in the stove so I could have a hot shower. This probably went on for an hour. I felt bad for the trees, but I needed it. I was in a really, really bad place. It was horrible.

There was this other woman who taught me to scrape off burnt dough from the cookie sheet to relieve stress. I'm pretty sure she was a witch. We danced a lot, but she hated being near cigarettes.

I remember walking down a trail one day, and this girl was walking behind me, but it was really quiet, so I started whistling "Hey Jupiter" by Tori Amos because that was when I was convinced I was quantumly connected to the planet Jupiter. She laughed. I don't know why. I never told anyone there that my name was Jupiter, even though Neptune called himself Neptune. He was really nice.

I don't know if they're all role-playing or if there are really gods there. My friend that took me there says he's an elf, but he's not very tall, and he doesn't really have pointy ears. It's just kind of a weird place, but very, very beautiful. I heard a kid self-immolated there once, though, so that kind of sucks. I've thought about self-immolating before, though–for sure. I thought I made a deal with the god of Zoroastrianism to get rid of all the bad thoughts in my brain. But I felt it happening, and it felt really weird in my brain, so I asked Fire to stop. Oh yeah, I stayed in the goat barn, and there's a sign that says "no flames". I felt like a flame.

This woman they call "granny" who lives there told me a lot of shit. First, I was outside looking for a cigarette, and someone gave me something to hit. I walked in the kitchen after feeling really, really fucked up and zombified, and Granny looked at me and said, "Wormwood." I guess I had smoked wormwood.

We went outside, and Granny gave me some real tobacco and started talking to me. She talked for probably an hour, but I was too fucked up to remember what she said. I do know that she talked about aliens, and I remember her saying that the best way they control us is through food.

By the way, in the room I was staying in in the goat barn there were pictures of Baphomet and shit. One guy I met who went there said he worshiped the "horned god". I guess that's who he was talking about–I don't really know. My granddaddy raised goats for some reason. I thought I was going to be some kind of sacrifice or something, so it was pretty scary.

After the eclipse happened (which was great–this really cute guy with a tarot card tattoo got naked and howled at the moon), they built this big fire, and hundreds of people probably gathered around in little groups. I stood by the fire because the whole time I was in severe pain, and it helped a lot.

Then, this is when it gets weird: They threw this piece of wood shaped like a goat's head on the fire, and all of the sudden my thoughts started being in sync with all the different conversations. Like, I would walk around to different groups, and they would give me things, and I would tell them things. It was so weird. I felt like a shaman or something. They were also playing these African drums or something, which was cool.

Oh, and one time I heard this beautiful piano music coming from the house. It made me feel like I took an opiate, it was so good. I followed the sound and found this guy who looked like a vampire playing the piano. I sat and listened for a while, and then the thought popped into my head that he was using a glamor on me or something. As soon as I thought that, he started playing terribly–forgetting notes. That was weird.

I usually felt really uncomfortable on the mountain, so I'd frequently walk down to the holler. It was so beautiful and peaceful down there. There's this beautiful stream with a waterfall, and the water is so clean and clear and refreshing. There was also this sign that said "Temple of the Unknown Goddess" with a bench beside it. I sat there a lot. There was a fruit tree with one piece of perfect fruit hanging from it. It kind of looked like a pear. Anyway, I'd go down there and just cry and release all my tension. It was a sad but beautiful and wonderful place.

I miss it. I thought the "Unknown Goddess" was the Mother Goddess aka Holy Spirit or something. It made sense because the holler connected two other camps–Ida, named after the Greek mountain of goddesses and a Christian camp with horses. I kind of always hoped a horse would come and take me away, but that never happened.

I should probably tell you about the resonance feelings, too, since I'm getting pretty close to 60,000 words.

The resonance feeling feels like a silk shit or spirit resting on me and through me. I don't know how else to describe it, but it is triggered by certain things I hear and think. I never can really predict what is going to trigger it.

One of the first times I remember getting it was when I was in bed thinking about my neighbor, who I thought was the reincarnation of Jonathan to my David. The next day he told me that at the same time that happened he had a vision of me giving him a blowjob.

One of the next times I had it, I was at a psychiatric hospital (long fucking story–too traumatic to tell right now), and I looked at this doctor, and the word "Brahman" popped in my mind. I got the resonance feeling that he was one, even though I didn't really know what it meant. I asked him if he was, and he nodded his head really quickly and told me we needed to work on me first. I don't know if he didn't want anyone to know or if he was just shocked that I knew.

I also got it last year that the borders were going to close. This was before Covid happened. Oh wait, I guess it would've been the year before last. Yeah. I also got it that there was going to be an ice age, but that hasn't happened.

It "told" me that me that it was the "Mother Goddess", Shakinah in Judaism, Sakina in Islam, Shakti in Hinduism, and Spirit of Truth in Christianity, which John says will only speak what it hears (which is basically what has been happening. I don't know, though). I just don't know. But yeah, that happens.

Man, Eve gave me a huge Reese's bar that's cut into rectangles, but I don't feel like eating, even though I haven't eaten all day.

Okay, I have officially eaten one nibble of Reese's bar today. That is enough. The music stopped, and I don't know why. Maybe I need to pick a new playlist or something. Oh wait, it was on pause. Courtney Love is playing again. I love her. I'd really like to hang out with her.

I wouldn't mind it if Courtney read my book. People give her a lot of shit, so I'm sure she wouldn't judge me as much as most. Hell, a lot of people think she killed the love of her life. Yva knew Kurt. She said it was a suicide–that he was just a suicidal person. She said he would've made out with me at a party. I can totally see that happening. I have a feeling Courtney wouldn't mind.

I also want Margot from The Magicians to hang out with Hale and Kate Bush and me. I doubt this will ever get popular, though. Oh, well. I really hope my family does find out what I've written, though. That would be terrible. By the way, when my mom pointed to her vagina and said, "Get in here", sne claimed she was talking about "Getting in the light", whatever that means. I don't know. I feel bad about talking shit. I should. I'm definitely going to change all the names at some point.

I love my family. I do. I love them. We're just very, very different people. But we're all kind of fucked up in our own way. I know they love me, too, even though it definitely doesn't feel like it sometimes. At least my mom is basically over me being gay. My dad isn't, so we just don't talk about it. Now the thing that they hate about me is my mental illness and drug use, which is also a symptom of mental illness. They hate me for that sometimes. It's mostly because I talk about crazy shit and ask weird questions that no one can answer about religion and stuff. My mom told me the Lord was going to strike me down and that snakes were going to come in my room. She also said he'd give me a stroke and that when they're in Heaven I'll be in Hell. I've said a lot of fucked up shit too, before, though.

Oh, when I was looking at porn I thought about the time I freaked out because I had been looking at an supposedly legal site that seemed to have slightly underage twinks on it. I sent a link to a cop friend, and he basically told me not to worry about it. I was worried that it was a sting operation or something, even though it wasn't on the Dark Web or anything. I was on a lot of Adderall then, though, I think. I did a lot of crazy shit on Adderall.

Eve's dad liked my music. I mostly made up stuff, but I also Played Battle Hymn to the Republic. He said it sounded like something from the Civil War, and I told him that the Union used it as a fight song or something. That's what I heard, at least. I'm not verifying any of this as I type.

Should I go to rehab or not? Maybe I'll ask Paul. I'll send this to him once I hit 60,000 words, whenever that is. Let me calculate. Oh shit, I already passed 60,000. Damn. Okay, I guess I'll take a break for a while and see what Paul has to say if he actually reads this. I'm going to miss this, kind of. That's sad. Is this the end? Maybe I'll write an epilogue at some point. That's what I'll do. If you read this all, I love you. I really, really do. I hope you don't hate me. If you don't hate me, maybe we can be friends one day. That'll be cool. Goodbye.

CHAPTER XV

A lot has happened since I last wrote. I know I said I was going to write an epilogue, and I guess this is it. It's been over two years since that Purim. Yom Kippur begins at sundown tonight. I'm still debating on whether or not I'm going too fast. My Jewish friend from Israel invited me to come to his house in Cochran tonight to have Torah study, but I have a house call with my insurance company tomorrow. Plus I have only really cat napped for the past few days due to the meth I've been smoking. Please don't judge. Well, I guess you might've assumed as much if you finished reading my last book. Maybe this go round I'll try to write sober. I wonder if I can stay sober for the next two weeks. Daniel is talking to me right now, but I'm not paying attention to what he's saying. That's Daniel Gates. He was supposed to be my literary agent, but I fired him last night and e-mailed some other lady who represented some guy who wrote a book my friend Paul said reminded him of mine. Daniel is my roommate. We met in rehab. I'm not sure if I mentioned that last time. I'm not exactly sure what all I mentioned about most things, really. Oh well. Maybe you won't either.

Like I can't remember if I used paragraph indentions or not. There's a copy of my book in my bedroom, but I'm a little too lazy to go check right now. I actually read it a couple times. It's pretty good, but that might be because it's me. I feel the same about my own music. Come to think of it, I feel the same way about the smell of my own farts, sometimes, too. I guess that doesn't really say a whole lot. Or maybe it does. Regardless, I think I'm going to put paragraph indentations, even though I think they're pretty passed.

I should smoke some weed. I have a headache stemming from the cyst in my nostril from picking my nose entirely too much. I can't help it. It gets really dry in my room, I guess. That's my excuse, at least. I should probably also quit doing hard drugs. I'm just a product of my environment. I'll quit when everyone else quits—or at least whenever I get new friends, although I'd rather keep my friends and find a way for us to all be both happy and healthy at the same time.

So I guess I should mention that I'm living in Milledgeville now at Amy's. Amy is Lori #1's mother. Lori #2 isn't talking to me anymore, ever since I told her she could shove the Music Instrument Library up her cunt. It just came out. I felt bad shortly after. I was really high, and I was working on a poem for Adelaide's dad's funeral, and she told me (in a bitchy way) that she didn't want to hear about death. Oh yeah, Adelaide's dad passed away. Cancer. He was such a good man. He is missed. I'm hoping I'll be able to find the hat he gave me once I go through my things at my parents' house.

A lot has happened since I last wrote. I'm pretty sure I said that already. Oh, my Freewrite was stolen. Nicole moved to a different apartment complex, and some fancy clothes I got from Stitch Fix and my Freewrite were in a garbage bag in her old apartment. Someone broke in, and that's all they took. I called the pawn shop, and they told me that they could honestly say that nothing like that had "walked into the store". I realized after I hung up that they could've technically been telling the truth and still have had it, since my Freewrite technically couldn't work. Oh well. I just got my new-to-me Alphasmart Neo in the mail today. I'm loving it so far. The keyboard has pretty clicks, and the screen refresh rate is actually better than the Freewrite, not surprisingly, since it's LCD instead of eInk. Plus it only cost me $80, as opposed to the $400 I would've spent had the only person who was selling a used one online had accepted my offer. Maybe it's meant to be. Heidi at Freewrite did offer me a whopping 5% discount to buy a new one, though. Still, that's four times my monthly rent payment.

There's this black author lady on YouTube who turned me on to the Alphasmart ecosystem. I really like the way she talks. She should definitely think about doing audio versions of her books if she hasn't already. I should tell her that. Oh, apparently Astrohaus, the makers of Freewrite, bought the Alphasmart name. So I guess I'm still representing. Thanks, Heidi. Sorry for slightly dissing your discount. Anyway, enough ambitious promotion.

Daniel handed me a fat joint he brought back from Turkey's. I took a few hits, and now I'm really thirsty, but I think I might've left my Mountain Dew in my car. Daniel is on the phone with his dad talking about his cryptocurrency shenanigans, which may or may not completely change our lives. Or it could be a scam or opportunist scheme at best. Time will tell. I'll write more about that later, maybe. Meanwhile, I'm going to go scouting for my drink before I thirst to death.

Okay, I didn't feel like walking to my car, so I got a Coca Cola and came to the porch, where I'm smoking a Lucky Strike Menthol Silver 100. The girls at the gas station down the road are great. They have funky, colorful hair and let me have things for free sometimes because I go in there pretty much every day. Oh yeah, I still haven't quit smoking cigarettes or wasting my seed. I have a lot to atone for this year, as usual. Maybe I should fast. I probably should fast. I definitely should fast, assuming there is a god who would want me to fast or find it endearing or something. Is it still considered fasting if you drink meal replacements? Probably not. I'm already hungry, but I don't feel like eating. Amy's going to make fish sticks and tater tots for supper, and I'm really looking forward to that. It's kosher, at least.

I came back inside, and I was bragging about how awesome this baby is. Daniel thought I was talking about a person. I had him type his name to see how the keyboard felt. He liked it.

167

He was amazed when he had me type something to see how fast I typed. The sentence was, "The dog went to the moon." I typed it in about two seconds. I've been able to type well over 130 wpm since I became obsessed with chatting on IRC in the mid-90s. AfterNET. #TheCow and #Rainbowroom. #TheCow belonged to my first and last "real" girlfriend, Susan, who sells things in England, I think. #Rainbowroom was the creation of Alli, the child psychologist who sent me roses and made a pact with me that we would get married at 23 if we hadn't already, but she did. Oh well. I ended up being very gay, anyway. I did write about a song about what would've happened otherwise. I mean, my most recent ex-boyfriend (new to you, unless you've known me since the last book) has a biological child and claims to be completely gay. He said the secret is viagra and lots of gay porn. I just don't think my imagination is active enough for that kind of ejaculation. And if I were to marry a woman, I'd want to procreate.

Oh yeah, Susan. I have a vivid memory of Susan and I making out in the living room of my childhood home to Matchbox 20's "Push". That was her idea, for some reason. If you pay attention to the lyrics, it's a bit odd, but whatever. Her then-closeted best friend Tommy stacked chairs up against the side of bedroom in hopes of catching us in some sort of act. Unfortunately for him, I couldn't even get it up. I've never been able to get it up for a girl, no matter how awesome and/or beautiful they may have been. I'm uncertain if it's a biological or environmental phenomenon (or something else), but I would really like to know. Maybe my soul is just from the feminine side. The Kabbalists say Isaac's was, too, before the sacrificial offering. That's why his mother laughed when she found out she was pregnant with him. The Kabbalists have very interesting insights and interpretations about things. I also read that David's soul was from the feminine side, but I don't understand that, since supposedly it can prevent one from procreating. Isaac was supposedly given a masculine soul after the incident on Mount Moriah. Please don't quote me on any of this. I'm not verifying anything as I type. I never do. That's how I roll.

Speaking of rolling, I need to decide if I'm going to have a drug theme for this book. Maybe I'll just play it by ear. Maybe I'll really try to stay sober while I write it. I'm sure people might be interested in how such an "addled" mind might work above the influence of substances. Wait, is "above the influence" the direct opposite of "under the influence"? It should be. It is now, if it's not. It's nice not having to Google things. It's like being in the 90s again and just making shit up.

I was just looking at Amy's coffee cup and thinking about how it looks like it says "Raw Rats" backwards and upside down. I'd watch that. I prefer a universe that has a holodeck, anyway. Oh, speaking of holodecks, we briefly had two Meta Quests. That was interesting. The Metaverse is pretty fun, albeit mostly underage and cliquey. Daniel pawned them and bought drugs, though. It was fun while it lasted.

I actually was thinking about starting my own world if Daniel's crypto thing pays off. I wrote an ambiguously tongue-in-cheek marriage proposal song to the Princess of Orange mentioning how our offspring could inherit the titles of two different worlds. That would be neat. I sent it to my friend Amanda, who claims she's going to forward it to her uncle, who is friend's with the King of England's brother, but we'll see. I think it could potentially be a pleasant little errand in light of the King's grieving to pass it along to his cousin, but on the other hand they could all just think I'm a mentally ill commoner, which isn't untrue.

Amy's phone is ringing, but she's not answering. Either it's a telemarketer or she's in the bathroom. She only has two or three people who call her, one of whom is her half-sister that I just found for her on AncestryDNA. Amy was adopted, and she knew nothing of her biological family except for her daughters. I found lots of information about her family, including a book her father (or grandfather—not entirely sure yet) wrote. He was an important Lebanese-American community leader. And Amy and her sister have been talking on the phone daily. I am so happy for them. Daniel was adopted, too, and I found his mom's first cousin in France, but the prospects of any sort of relationship seem kind of lackluster. It's okay, though, since Daniel doesn't seem too interested about the idea of connecting with biological family, anyway. I love it, though. I keep hoping I'll find a half-sibling in Vietnam one day. My dad did have a "hooch maid" there, whatever that entails. I just know she was paid with a wheelbarrow of their money.

Ugh, I took a couple hits of a DMT vape the other day, and I still get random phantom smells of it. It definitely seems like it came from some sort of animal's gland. I didn't feel any effects, though. I don't know why. Maybe my brain is already overloaded with it. That would explain a lot. Oh yeah, there's something I should share about my potentially supernatural experiences, as it is relevant to what I've been writing about, but I don't really want to bring it up right now. It's kind of a disappointment. Well, it's a potential disappointment. It could be nothing. It depends on your threshold for probabilistic determinations, or something like that, I guess.

Okay, so, I think I may have mentioned the resonance feeling in my last book. It's this physical sensation that flows through my body when I hear or think certain things, mostly of theological or apparent prophetic nature. Well, it seemed like I got it when I found Amy's step-sister on AncestryDNA that it was actually an aunt-niece relationship. Theoretically, it could be, but that would mean that there was an extraordinary amount of inbreeding in their father/grandfather's line. I do know that the father/grandfather married his first cousin, but there had to have been more than that. Also, that would mean that the guy who wrote the book was Amy's grandfather, and his son was Amy's father. I don't know any way of ever finding out without exhuming some bodies. Oh well.

Oh, another thing the resonance feeling told me was that the Russian Nationalist organization that is controlling part of the Ukraine right now will be taking over the Ukraine by the end of the year. This information came from the resonance feeling I got that was triggered by a Marilyn Manson song that described the Russian-backed government's flag colors: blue, black, and red. So, I guess we'll see. I don't want to be a false prophet, though. And then, I wonder: What if I'm changing the timeline with what I'm doing with this knowledge? You never really know with the butterfly effect. But it seems pretty futile to dwell on such hypotheticals. Still, I just don't want to be labeled a false prophet. That's just one more reason for which some think I should die, according to some interpretations of Torah law. Fortunately, even if the Sanhedrin (Jewish court) existed, capital punishment can only be carried out if the perpetrator has been warned by two unrelated witnesses and continues to commit the violation. And if they do continue, then they are considered insane, since no sane person would risk death for breaking a commandment, and you can't execute an insane person. So even one instance of capital punishment in seventy years, according to the sages, would be considered a murderous court. I fucking love Judaism. L'Chaim. I just asked Daniel if he's going to fast, and he said he would, so I guess I am, too. At least I have a little meth in my system. That should help. I'll fill up on fish sticks and tater tots soon enough. I asked Amy if she could make them before sundown, and asked sarcastically if we were being Jewish again. I guess we are.

Now she and Daniel are talking about whether or not Turkey and his girlfriend think she's a bitch for wanting them to come back and finish cleaning the house since we paid them $200 and they've only done the kitchen, living room, and bathroom. They still have to do her bedroom and bathroom, but she doesn't wake up until the afternoon. Oh, Turkey's girlfriend said I could write about her, but she said to call her "nothing". So, Turkey and Nothing are cool people. They're pretty much the only people I hang out with in this town anymore. They also said I could write anything about them, which is cool. I suck at remembering to censor myself, obviously. Well, I assume it's obvious, at least.

Okay, I came outside to smoke another cigarette. But before I did, I went into the kitchen, and Amy said I seemed happy and like I was doing good. She said she was happy about that. She has no idea I smoked some meth, though. Honestly, it's really no different than when I was prescribed Adderall. I don't do that much. Maybe I should stop making excuses. Drugs are bad, mmkay. Everything is a drug. Love is a drug. Love is the worst drug there is for me. It's also the best drug. Hell, it's the reason I ended up in the psychiatric hospital a couple weeks ago.

Oh, I realized when I was reading my last book that I never really went into detail about my psychiatric hospital experiences. I don't really know why. Wait, did I mention the guy who accused me of rape? What about the guy who stole my underwear and pooped in them? My memory is so terrible. Should I search through my book to see if I've already written about things before I try to write about them again? I don't want to annoy anyone by repeating things. But I also want this to be as close to stream-of-consciousness as possible without being incomprehensible. Speaking of consciousness, there's a song I recorded last night that I need to rewrite. An old friend of mine is going to record drums with it. He has a record label called Divine Mother Records, which I just found out about today, I think. It's pretty significant for me, since the resonance feeling claims to be from the mother goddess, also known as "Shekinah", "Shakti", "Sakina", and the one who spoke through the serpent in the Garden of Eden, interestingly. But then again, it could just be my fucked up psyche or neurological system. Who knows?

Oh cool, I just found out I can change the font size on my Alphasmart. That's pretty cool. I changed it to small, and now it's perfect. I really like this device, although if I can find a literary agent who can help me sell enough books to buy one, I might still get a Freewrite eventually. Actually, I'm kind of interested in what Astrohaus's version of the Alphasmart's keyboard is going to feel like. Maybe this book will get popular enough so that they'll send me a free one. Famous people always get free shit. I don't want to be super famous, though. Jupiter Davidson can be underground famous for his books and music, but I don't really want to be recognized in public or anything. That would probably suck. I like anonymity. It's nice. Oh, I showed my nephew a little paragraph in my last book where I mentioned him and his family, and he said they loved me. I needed to hear that. I've been missing family a lot lately. At night I fantasize about my childhood days at grandma and granddaddy's house before I fall asleep. It's a lot better than the random flashes of penises I usually get after binge-watching porn and regretting it.

The neighbor across the street is checking his mail with this little girl. That's sweet. I wish I were stable enough to have a child. It's a bit of a Catch 22, though, I think. In order to have a child, I need to be stable, but the best way to be stable would be to have a child. That's what a lot of less-than-responsible people say after they have kids, at least. I think they're on to something. Too bad I can't just randomly knock someone up. I still have a slight curiosity about how my sexuality would react to the presence of stereotypical female genitalia on a transitioning male who would be willing to carry a fetus. I have an old friend who is a trans woman, and she was on Ricki Lake many years ago for having children with her trans husband. This was back when the myth was still going around that Walt Disney left a condition in his will that the first man to have a child would inherit Disney World. Too bad that was bullshit. They could've done great things.

I just took a picture of what I wrote and sent it to Bianca. I hope she doesn't mind. I don't think she will. Whether or not she's still with the same guy, I have no idea, though. That's the thing about assuming. As my eighth grade teacher Mrs. Lancaster said, it makes an ass out of you and me. I wonder if she's still alive. I should Google her someday. Ugh, the last time I Googled teachers at my school, I found out that there was one single teacher left who taught when I was in high school, and had just started when I was there. I'm so old. Lane said my writing sounded like someone very young who had amassed years worth of memories, though. That probably has something to do with my low emotional intelligence, though.

Sundown is in 45 minutes, and Amy is just now starting to cook. I should start wrapping up this chapter, too. I'm not sure if it's appropriate to work on Yom Kippur. I mean, it's not the Sabbath. And I'm not even Jewish, yet, anyway, as far as I know. I mean, maybe my soul is Jewish. Maybe my maternal lineage is Jewish if you go far enough back, but I can't prove it in a rabbinic court. My mitochondrial haplogroup K is most pronounced in Ashkenazi populations, though, which is pretty cool, I think.

Okay, I ate some fish sticks and tots, and now I'm watching Rabbi Friedman talk about Yom Kippur after sharing Leonard Cohen's "Who by Fire" with Daniel. By the way, Daniel wants me to refer to him by his full name, Daniel Gates. I'm not sure why, but there you go. I wonder if there is anyone with whom I should make amends that I haven't already. I don't think there is, but I could be wrong. Oh yeah, Lori #2. I should apologize again—I think I have to do it one more time before I'm forgiven by default. I'm going to call her now.

Okay, her voicemail says she lost her phone, so I left her a message. I hope she calls me sometime. I really miss her and the Music Instrument Library. She and it have the potential to really help people. I mean, they already have. They helped me. Oh yeah, I should tell you the story about the time I was houseless, if I haven't already. I don't know if I have, to be honest. I wish my memory were more functional. I also should tell you all that has happened in the past two and a half years, if I can even remember. It's kind of a blur. I'm totally ignoring Rabbi Friedman. My bad. He has his book displayed behind him. That was such a great read. I should take his class again. Too bad he's so popular—otherwise, I'd try to get him to be my rabbi. He did tell me he thinks it would be better for me to convert so I could do more mitzvot.

Meanwhile, the sun is about to be down, so I guess I'm going to end this chapter. I was going to write one chapter per day, but Amy said I should just pop my soul out while it's going. But I like taking breaks every now and then. I also need to get some sleep tonight—more than a cat, at least. Oh, Nicole got a new puppy. She is so adorable. Did you know puppies sleep about 20 years per day? I need to sleep like a puppy and catch up. I highly doubt that will happen, though. Also, that would be kind of cheating if I'm going too fast. Rabbi Friedman says our remorse and regret is life-changing and life-giving, so I think I'm going to smoke another cigarette and then go lie down in my bed, where I'll attempt to conjure up those kinds of emotions about all the naughty things I've done like masturbate. And I'll try not to masturbate.

CHAPTER XVI

Well, it's daytime again, and I still haven't slept. Thanks, meth. This is terrible. What am I doing with my life? Oh yeah, as soon as the sun went down I masturbated, too. And I've been chain-smoking on top of that. The other day I heard a rabbi say it was basically pointless to try to be Jewish unless you live in a Jewish community, what with the lack of accountability and all. I'm currently lying in an extremely uncomfortable position on my bed and listening to my new album on SoundCloud. It's also on all the various streaming services. It's called Frequency, and the album art is a photograph of my great-great grandparents. The wife was a medicine woman, but I like to think she was a witch because that sounds a little more interesting.

My entire body is in moderate to severe pain right now. I think I'm going to take some Kratom. I'm out of Neurontin, and I don't think Walmart is going to fill my prescription since I missed my psychiatrist appointment. I wish I could be okay without drugs. I'm such a mess. Kratom it is.

Ugh, it's so nasty. The powder form is bad. But it's better than being in pain. I really need to start taking my psychiatric medication again. I'm going to do that right now, actually. Abilify, Cymbalta, and Wellbutrin. That's the first time I've taken my meds in days. Well, I took everything except the Wellbutrin, at least. I'm not really sure what I did with them. Besides, there was a study that came out recently that said antidepressants basically have no effect on depression anyway, I think. So there's that. God, I'm so gassy.

Yeah, so two years later, and I'm still debating on going to rehab. "God bless America, home of the free, where you can be a crazy junkie, too, just like me." That's a lyric to a song of mine that was just playing. Appropriate. I was actually considering going to Sweden or Germany or some other country with a better mental health system and registering as a humanitarian refugee before I end up offing myself either accidentally or on purpose. I've come extremely close. Did you know that after being hospitalized ten times for suicidal ideation, I still haven't gotten a case manager, even though I've requested one? Oh, and a few weeks ago when I was suicidal, Facebook banned me from going live. I guess they didn't want anyone to see me kill myself. They didn't even give me the option to call anyone for help. Fuck Zuckerberg.

Now one of my songs is taunting me about sleep. I wish I could sleep. Sleep would be amazing. I wish I could sleep forever. That would be ideal. Waking life is for the birds. Mammalian brains shouldn't be forced to deal with this horrible existence. I wish we could all crawl back into our respective mothers' wombs, non-sexually, of course.

Anyway, the Kratom has started to kick in, and I feel a little bit better. I think I might take a nap for a little bit after I pee. I was just talking with my friend Steven about the number of our (real) full names in Hebrew. His is 611, which is the number for "Torah", and mine is 541, the number for "Israel". If you subtract the two, you get 70, which is a very special number. According to Chabad, there are ten significant instances of seventy including seventy holy days and seventy "faces" or perspectives of understanding the Torah. That's pretty neat. Steven was always one of the most Jewish non-Jews I knew, so I'm not surprised, really. Okay, time to pee and then nap, hopefully.

Well, I slept for an hour or two, and the lady from my insurance company came over for a house call visit. She was really nice, and she gave me a set of kitchen spatulas and oven mitts. Now I'm sitting on the front porch having a forbidden Yom Kippur cigarette, even though she just told me I was wheezing when she listened to my breathing. I'm still sleepy, though. And I really don't want this cigarette. I think I'm going to play Worlds and go back to bed.

"Three Rounds and a Sound" by Blind Pilot is playing. It's dark now—well after midnight. I'm stoned. I feel a lot better. Fuck meth. Soil and six feet under. Daniel and I were just talking— well, I was just talking—about whether or not I was going to have a funeral and what song I wanted to play at it. First I wanted "Yellow Ledbetter" by Pearl Jam (which reminded me of an old friend of mine who shared the name), but then I thought about "Joan of Arc" by Leonard Cohen if I were to be cremated. But then "Running to the Edge of the World" by Marilyn Manson sounded more appealing and more ironic. I like all of them, really. I think all of them should be played. For sure. Or is that too much? That's probably too much. Too much. That reminds me of the time when the girl with the green eyes couldn't stop laughing and yelling that it was too much when I was writhing on the floor and licking it after the doctors told me I wasn't crazy or something. That was when I let some crack head steal my car because I thought she was taking me to sacrifice me in Helen.

Anyway, I don't feel like triggering my PTSD at this very moment —maybe later. Fuck, I have so many things I should probably tell you, but I'm such a pussy—no offense to pussies, real or imagined. Does that sound sexist? I apologize in advance. Well, it's advanced for me, at least. Deep beneath the cover of another perfect wonder where it's so white as snow. I love this song. I'm not going to tell you what it is because if you know, you know. If you don't know, you should find out. Or not. It's up to you. You can do whatever you want. It's your life. It's your veins. The choice is yours. Fuck, that reminds me of Whit. He wrote that about me in a song once—the song he composed using the suicide note I sent him. Whit is the one who introduced me to Yva Las Vegass, my old roommate who was in the band with Krist Novoselic, the guy from Nirvana. Yes, I'm name-dropping for context. Yva and I are good again. I'm glad. I missed her. She's good people.

Why do I keep getting emails that Neil Gaiman tweets? I don't really care. I don't even use Twitter. My friend Craig is friends with Neil. I think I asked him to try to get a message to Tori Amos for me through Neil back when I thought the muses were communicating information about me to her, but he said he hadn't heard from him in a while. Craig asked me for money the other day. I guess that was him, at least. I hope he's okay. I'm just poor as fuck at the moment. I need new teeth so bad. The dentist quoted me over $9000 for partial dentures. Yeah, right.

CHAPTER XVII

Well, I ended up passing the fuck out finally. Daniel and I are smoking our second bowl of weed. Amy just went to her bedroom. She was recalling her days as a prison guard. I think our roommate dynamics are pretty good. Amy is a sane former prison guard and Daniel is a crazy former inmate. And I'm somewhere in between, I think. I'm stoned. Amy is making Mexican rice. I just ate a banana sandwich with mayo. I'm pretty full. I think I'm going to go smoke cigarettes in the sun. I like writing better when I'm high.

I spoke with Lori #2 on the phone for a while. She forgives me. She and her daughter Prairie are in South Dakota trying to make their way to NYC. I'm trying to help them find the cheapest mode of transportation. I might meet them up there if Yva will let me stay with her, maybe. We'll see. I haven't seen Yva in years, but I saw Lori earlier this year when my mom and I flew out to LA for a week. That was kind of a disaster. Oh yeah, I should probably tell you about that. So far I need to tell you about the guy who accused me of rape and my trip to LA with my mom. Or maybe I already told you about the guy in my last book? I keep forgetting I need to look in my book for these things. I'm just so incredibly lazy and forgetful. I have to poop now. So that's what I'm going to do.

Alright, it's been a few hours. I ended up coming to Cochran. I'm at Nicole's. I'm a little upset, though. I had messaged Yva and told her I may be going to live in NYC for a while next year since Bear is getting an artist residency there and invited me. I told her they kind of remind me of each other (in good ways), and she sent me a voice message talking about how that sounds racist or some shit, and she has no tolerance for racism, and that if we are going to be friends again, we have to take it slow.

This is the same bitch who kicked me out in the middle of the night for quoting an article about how a higher percentage of free black people owned slaves during the civil war than white people. Fortunately a homeless black couple took me in and took care of me. A while later, my black roommate confirmed the article was correct when he informed me that his black ancestors owned slaves. Oh, and she lost her contract with Krist Novoselic in the 90s because she thought he was racist. Anyway, it sucks because I really thought we were going to be friends again. When everything is good, it's great. It's just her obsession with hating white people or assuming we're all racist or something. It doesn't work. Bear just messaged me. I think I'm going to vent to them. Hopefully these pain pills will kick in soon.

I don't know why people are being such dicks today. They're fucking with my buzz. This other guy messaged me and was being an ass, but I don't feel like going into it right now. Let's just say he used to be a very good friend until he found out I stole his (ugly) dick pic from his phone when I was drunk and horny after he let me give him a massage while he was shirtless and kissing me on my arm. It just really makes me angry when people I care about hurt me. It makes me want to hurt them. Let's hope I don't end up being a serial killer or something. No, this is not foreshadowing. I wouldn't be terribly disappointed if the world ended, though, through no means of my own. It's all kind of bullshit, really. On a positive note, Nicole's pup is lying beside me. She's a good dog.

CHAPTER XVIII

Well, I guess opiates aren't very conducive to my prolificacy. Did I just make that word up? Anyway, I'm back in Milledgeville sitting in the living room, also known as Daniel's room, while he's listening to an audiobook about Hermes Trismegistus. I got denied by another rabbi the other day, and on the way home today I called this conservative rabbi in Macon who denied me and left him a very honest but harsh message. He really hurt me by lying to me and ghosting me, even though he claimed he didn't ghost me once I sent him an aggressive article. But I still haven't heard from him either since the spring of this year or last—I don't know it's been a while, though. Daniel wants to know if I'm hungry for some hot dogs. I don't know. Sure.

I just checked my old book and noticed where I didn't use paragraph indentations, and I put a line between each paragraph. I like the aesthetics of that, so I guess I'm going to be editing some. That's unfortunate. Or will I? Should I? I know it annoys some people if I do, but it would annoy others (maybe more similar people to me) if I didn't. Damned if I do, damned if I don't. That's life in this dualistic world when you're a transcendental catwoman. I don't know. I really don't. All I know is that if I were a rabbi, I'd be a little worried that someone might go on to birth a new Amalek if I rejected them for conversion. If you're a Talmudic scholar, you know what I mean (or you will). I was really hoping the rabbi would've asked for forgiveness on Yom Kippur. That would've been a fucking miracle.

I've been feeling very homicidal today. It's kind of disturbing. I don't think I'd really kill anyone, but I have short little fantasizes about running people over if they happen to appear in front of me while I'm driving down the highway. Daniel says it's not illegal for me to say that, as long as I don't say I'm going to do it. I'm not going to do it. I don't have a plan. This isn't my first rodeo, though it's always been with myself.

So the rabbi volunteers to feed the homeless in Macon for one of his mitzvot, But he said he called the cops on one of the homeless men for knocking on his door once. He's kind of a piece of shit, in my opinion. He makes hot sauce that is bland, and he named his son after a holy book. He calls himself the gatekeeper to Judaism. Goddamnit, Amy just got pissed off because I told her I was busy when she kept trying to interrupt me while I was typing to tell me she bought some banana nut muffins. I just wish the fucking planet would explode.

Anyway, back to the stupid fucking rabbi. I really liked him at first. He told me he was going to "walk up the mountain with me" to learn Torah. I was so excited. I waited patiently the next week because that's when he said we'd start, but I never heard from him. After sending him a couple polite queries, I finally decided he was ghosting me and sent him an article about how calling yourself a gatekeeper just makes you an asshole, which I think is true. My social work advisor said that to me, too, when she said I had to fix my mental health before she would let me be a social worker. Fucking cunt. Goddamn, these people are going to turn me into a terrorist. This must be what Hitler felt like when he was rejected as an artist. We have the same birthday according to the Julian calendar. My mother went into labor on Yom Hashoah, though, and gave birth to me right at sunset. Yom Hashoah is Holocaust Remembrance Day. The number of my name in Hebrew is 541, which is the same as "Israel". My mom's birthday is May 14, and my dad was born in 1948. Israel was founded May 14, 1948. These are a few pieces of possible evidence I had that I may have had a Jewish soul, although I know many would say there's no such thing as "possible evidence". I would disagree with them, though. Again, if the planet exploded, I'd be okay with that. I'd be like Kirsten Dunst in Melancholia. I met her once when I was on shrooms in Venice Beach. She pulled out a bottle of perfume from her Louis Vuitton purse and sprayed it with me and laughed. We were sitting in a circle, and there were people taking pictures of us, but I'm not sure if they were paparazzi or if I accidentally sat down in the middle of a shoot. Anyway, she was nice.

I want to run away. I wish I had that kind of money. Oh, I smoked some Delta 9 THC or something. That's what Daniel said it was. It's from Amy's ex. I think it's actually Delta 8. Anyway, I'm just in a shittie mood. I think it's my borderline acting up. I also have to poop, but I like to shower after I poop, and there's a bunch of water stuck in the tub. I'll just ask Daniel if he'll fix it since he did it. Okay, he's fixing it.

I have absolutely no appetite, either. Maybe I should start taking my medicine again, even if it makes me fat. I guess being fat is sexy now. I was actually at a gay campground recently, and apparently being thin is a bad thing there. People kept talking shit about anyone who wasn't fat. Maybe I should go back to a psych ward or a rehab. Oh wait, UnitedHealthcare let me switch my insurance without fucking informing me that I would lose my rehab benefits just to get $2000 in dental insurance when it takes fucking $9000 to get my teeth fix at the only place who will take it. So no rehab for me unless I drop it and wait until next month. Again, world explode, please.

Maybe this will be my suicide book. I think that's a great idea. Maybe my soul can feed on the guilt of all the assholes left behind. Whatever. I think every goddamn fetus should be aborted immediately to prevent anyone from having a life remotely as shittie as mine. I'm going to buy more Kratom. Fuck this. Fuck this book.

Okay, Daniel and I went to town and got some Kratom. I feel a little better. My car seems like it's about on its last leg, though. It makes this really bad knocking noise a lot. I think it's a coil or something. I'm waiting for my dead boyfriend's dad to get a settlement because he said he's going to fix my car for me, which is really sweet. Oh yeah, I've felt extremely guilty about mentioning him in a slightly negative light in my last book. He is a great man. I guess it wasn't really negative or anything, but it could be taken that way. Plus I was upset at the time. I'm okay now. Maybe I'll feel the same way about the rabbi one day. If only.

Am I that terrible of a person? I definitely feel like it sometimes. If someone wants to put me out of my misery, please just be humane about it. That's all I ask. And preferably don't let me know it's coming.

I should stop being so morbid. I have to pee. I don't really want to die at the present moment. I'm okay, I guess. I just don't have that much to say, but I also don't know what else to do with myself. I'm so bored. I mean, there are things I haven't told you about that I could tell you about, but I'm too lazy to dig up anything out of my memories at the moment. If it comes up, it comes up. But I don't have the motivation to force anything up. I definitely have to pee. I'm going to go pee.

Much better. "Got You Where I Want You" by The Flys is playing on Apple Music. I like this song. It makes me feel nostalgic. I miss the 90s. That was a good decade. I haven't really written about the 90s much, have I? Hell, I don't remember. I saw Jett today. She's from the 90s. She was in my little group along with Lilly and Randall, my best friend who was murdered. I wonder if Lilly has read my book yet. I doubt it. She is so responsible and busy with work and her family and being a mom and stuff. I'm proud of her. I never thought she would've turned out that way. I imagined some bitter, drunken playwright in NYC or something. She used to drive with her feet. Nicole's kid made a comment about me driving with my knees earlier today when I was taking him to the store. I think that's where I got it from. Lilly is swell. She used to read the dictionary and channel Margaret Mitchell. We flipped my car once, and I thought we all died. I was okay with it and wanted to do it again. Good times, good times.

I think I'm going to play Civilization VI for a bit before I go to bed. I know this is a short chapter, but at least it isn't as short as the past two. Maybe I'll do better tomorrow.

CHAPTER XIX

Okay, it's tomorrow. I just asked Daniel what time it was, and he said it was 6:28. I'm pretty sure—yeah, I'm definitely sure it's 6:28 in the evening. I'm just a little stoned. Amy let me smoke some of her real weed. I've been smoking this Delta 8 shit all day. The only thing I do well on is real weed, I think. I feel a lot better now. I also wrote a new song about nuclear war and reincarnation. That was nice. My friend Brent liked it. I'm not sure if it fits the correct theme on Reddit, though. Oh, Amy's daughter Lori #1 and I spoke today. She says Reddit is full of bad people. I agree, but I told her this subreddit doesn't allow downvoting or negative remarks. At least I've never gotten any, other than a tongue-in-cheek "eww" when I posted a song about teenage sex. They still liked it, though.

Oh yeah, I don't want to have sex with teenagers anymore. I mean, I never really did—I just thought some were physically attractive. But I spent less than thirty minutes at my ex's daughter's homecoming party, and I changed my mind. Maybe it was just because they were all the popular kids, though. I don't know. Maybe it's just because I'm old. Old and weird. I'm an old, weird guy talking about sexual thoughts about teenagers. I still feel like it's a natural thing for males. Maybe it's because females are intuitive so you have to get them while they're young and naive. I don't know. Is that sexist? My bad. I'm not into young girls, though. I'm not even into young boys. I'm into guys who look like legal men who happen to be in high school. I think I was one of those at one point in my life, and I'm not traumatized by the old men who wanted to fuck me. I hit on someone about my age when I was a teenager. He was so hot. I couldn't believe he was in his 30s.

Fuck, I'm old. This sucks. I miss the 90s. I would do almost anything to be able to transport back into my 90s self in the 90s. It'd be cool if all my friends and family could. That would be amazing, actually. Hey, that would be a good plot for a Netflix series. I should pitch that to Paul. Oh, this guy Paul did some movies with—I forget his name at the moment, but he did a movie called Crash, I think—added me to Instagram. I thought it was kind of strange since as far as I know Paul and I have never been friends on there. I hardly ever even use it. Anyway, my Truman Show Syndrome flared up for a bit, needless to say for some.

Let's talk about kittens or something. I started feeling the anxiety well up in my chest. I'll ask Daniel what something good to write about is. He says "world peace". Bah humbug. I don't even know. How about world in pieces? World peace. World boring more like it. Thanks Daniel, you suck as a muse and as a literary agent. I love you, anyway. Oh, Daniel is technically a billionaire on paper in cryptocurrency on a U.S. registered exchange. He could buy some peace, I guess, for a little while at least. The holy dove is bought and sold and bought again. She is never free. Forget your perfect offering. Goddamn, I love Leonard Cohen. Speaking of light, I just had a resonance feeling. I'm having a large emotional response right now. The widowhood of every government, signs for all to see. You know we're on the last pope, right? But they've summoned up a thunder cloud, and they're gonna hear from me.

Fuck, Daniel and I both agree that we need some drugs. Does that make us codependent? Oh well. I just want some opiates. Oh wait, I could eat some Kratom, I guess. I ate some earlier today right after I ate some ribs from Shane's Rib Shack, which were delicious, but I had to swallow my puke. At least it was delicious pig butt puke I got to swallow or whatever. Oh wait, I guess pigs don't have ribs in their butts. My bad, pigs. The ribs were delicious. I highly recommend them. Just wait a while before you ingest tree leaf powder and try to chase it with sweet tea. I wish I had leftovers, but I split it with Amy. I'm sorry I might've said mean things about her yesterday. I was in a really pissy mood. That's what happens when I feel rejected, I guess. Plus I think the full moon had something to do with it, not to mention the fact that I accidentally typed "moon" instead of "mood" earlier and had to change it. I guess I forgot about Jungian synchronicity. I have to pee. I'm so lazy. I wish I could just pee myself and it'd be okay. I mean, I wish I could be okay with that kind of life. I'd need a lot of drugs, I guess. That's what they give you when you're dying. My friend Bear's brother died today. He was surrounded by his loved ones, which we agree is the best way you can go. They invited me to come stay with them for a while in NYC when they start their artist's residency there next year. That would be cool. Too bad Yva and I got into it again. She just pushes my buttons with this race-baiting bullshit or whatever it's called. She needs help. For real. Oh, I got pissed off and edited Sweet 75's Wikipedia entry to quote my book on their breakup. I wonder how long it'll take before she realizes it. It's fact, though—at least according to what I remember her telling me about the situation. Well, she also claimed he called her a "nigger" for stealing something from a gas station, which kind of makes me laugh in the way I'd laugh of someone I didn't like had something fucked up but not too bad happen to them. Anyway, whatever, she's not even black. That's stupid to break up a $3 million contract over something like that. Why not try to educate him if you think he's so ignorant? Whatever. She just likes being a bitch, I think. Maybe it's the adrenaline rush or something, but it's very triggering. Or maybe she has PTSD. Regardless, I don't understand why the fuck she takes it out on me of all people. If anything, it just makes me not like her.

Anyway, whatever. I'm a faggot, so I have the goddamn right to my observations and interpretations, goddamnit. If you don't think so, then we can't be friends. Sorry. Go fuck off. Anyway, Daniel says she shouldn't have been a nigger. Ha. God, please someone sue me so I can make a name for myself. Just kidding, I can't see anything positive coming from any of this other than this, but I live for the reviews. I do with music, too. I love feedback. It makes life worth living. I need drugs. Maybe I'll take more Kratom. Weed candy. That's what I need. Edibles. That's definitely what I need. I'm going to see if I can get some soon. Fruity pebbles, I think. I don't know. That was just some weird connection in my brain. I was about to mention something about jacking off, but I realized Daniel is sitting beside me, and even though I guess he can't read my thoughts, it'd still be weird going into detail about it even though I mention my masturbatorial conundrums to him all the time. I wish I could smoke cigarettes inside. I guess I can in my room at night. Amy said I could with the window open so I don't have to wake up Daniel to go out the door to smoke. I kind of abuse that privilege a lot.

I need to take my medicine. Maybe that would help me feel less bored. I wonder what I would be like if I took my medicine as much as I took my drugs. That would be an interesting experiment, perhaps. I don't know if I have the dedication to make it happen, though.

I just emailed Perez Hilton and told him I wrote a book with some celebrity gossip and that we met years ago at Akbar. I didn't tell him what my real name was, though. I just need to sell some more books. Daddy needs a new set of teeth. Meanwhile, I think I'm going to play some more Civilization VI again. I'm trying to win as Sweden.

Alright, I played for a while. I settled four cities, but I got bored. I was going for a cultural victory, as usual. A domination victory would probably be far more interesting, but I'm more of a pacifist, even though I have my moments. I'm listening to a song that mentions something about the singer's grandfather. It's a Manchester Orchestra song. I wish I would've gotten to know my grandfathers better. My dad's dad died when I was four, I think, but my mom's dad lived until I was in my twenties. I just didn't have very much to do with him since my grandma died. She was definitely the glue that held the family together, as is fairly common for Southern matriarchal cultures (and others). I learned when I was living on the Lakota Sioux reservation that the grandmas were the elders and raised the kids. That's pretty neat. I got temporarily healed by one when I had Syphilis once at a Rainbow Gathering in the Black Hills. That was a tumultuous event. Teepees are cool, though.

I apologize for the lack of a trigger warning for my previous comments, by the way. At the time it seemed humorous, but looking back I can see how some might not get my humor and be offended. Oh well. My bad. I don't really think it's nice for people to call people the n-word, just like I don't think it's nice for people to call people the f-word, although people do it all the time in jest.

I may have inadvertently created many more people I need to apologize to before next Yom Kippur, if I end up going back in the Judaism direction. We'll see. I know I said some harsh things about that rabbi yesterday, but my feelings were really hurt. It's the borderline. Black and white thinking. It's better to beat the fuck out of me than ignore me—literally, both have happened to me more than once.

Did I mention I would really like some drugs? Hard drugs would be nice—preferably an opiate. Heroin would be cool. I like heroin. It makes me feel really good, to say the least. I don't know why it's got such a terrible reputation. If you're going to be a junkie, but addicted to heroin. Just kidding. Don't be a junkie, kids. It's bad.

I wish you would stop back from my ledge, my friend. Yeah, let's do that. Thanks, Third Eye Blind. Maybe your third eye isn't so blind after all. Although I do wonder how many teenagers you got to try meth with your subconscious influence with your obvious but uncomprehended lyrics. I'd masturbate for the endorphins, but I don't feel like dealing with the guilt right now.

What genre is this? I put my last book under memoirs and biographies on Amazon, but I wonder if there is something more appropriate. I doubt it. I don't know what genre my music fits under, either. How sad. Doesn't help the feeling that I'm alone in the world. It'd be nice to find others like me in some specific way other than demographics. Demographics mean very little when it comes to some things. I need a cigarette.

I'm smoking one in my bed because I think it's late enough, even though Daniel is still awake. I have the fan on, and the window is open, so I don't think it's noticeable. I really like being able to smoke while I type. Oh, fuck, Tori is playing. She's your cocaine. Damn, I wouldn't mind someone who produced similar effects as cocaine, even though it's really not my favorite drug or anything.

My dad bought my mom a new laptop and gave me her old one. I should use it to upload what I've written so far in case something happens to my Neo. Neo. When did the Matrix come out? I'm sure it was before this thing was made. I'm sure whoever named it was aware of the movie. I do feel slightly outside of the Matrix when I write on it, since I'm not connected to the Internet or anything. I love that.

I should just buy a type A to C usb adapter for my MacBook. I need one anyway for my piano. I feel like I've been totally neglecting it in my music. It's just me and my shittie guitar skills. I should add my shittie piano skills to the mix. Maybe that would make it more interesting. Oh, my friend Brent gave me good feedback on the song I wrote today, but of course friends aren't usually going to be very critical. He's in a locally famous band. I'm going to try to make it to their Halloween show in Macon. Shout out to Choir of Babble. I apologize if you're ashamed to be mentioned in the same chapter as some of my off-color thoughts, no pun intended. I'd say I have black friends, but that makes you sound racist now. Fuck it. Think what you want. If you know me, you know.

Maybe this should be a suicide book. Too bad I'm such a pussy. Ugh, I ate some more Kratom. That shit tastes so fucking bad. Gross.

I'm listening to this last album I uploaded to all the streaming services. It's called "Frequency". I've decided to try to make each album sound a little bit better than the last, production-wise or whatever. We'll see how that goes. I had two albums on the Internet through Distrokid, but they removed them when I switched to SoundCloud. Oh well.

I wish I could remember enough about what I already wrote to know what I should write about. I have no idea, though, really. Maybe this shouldn't be a memoir. Maybe this should just be something else—a look into the addled mind of a blah blah blah. I've actually gotten some pretty decent reviews so far. Maybe I should tell everyone I'm really... Oh wait, no, I can't say that. It's too soon. Maybe I will in the third book. You can probably guess what I was going to say, anyway. Okay, maybe I'm really the god of thunder. Maybe I'm the reincarnation of David. Maybe I was Hitler in a past life. Maybe I was Jesus. Maybe I'm the moshiach. Maybe I'm just fucking insane. Either way, give me your money. Just kidding. Give me your reviews, though. I need them. I need them to like myself. Listen to my music, too, or find someone you think might like it. It's not for everyone.

,CHAPTER XX

If you've made it this far, let's talk about race. First of all,
what is race? It seems the common colloquial definition
derives from which population the majority of your ancestors
came from within the past few hundred years. I guess the
broadest definition would be those of Asian, European, and
African descent—at least those were correlated with the
sons of Noah from the Bible, I think. Japhetic, Semitic, and
African. According to the Table of Nations yDNA chart from
FamilyTreeDNA, my yDNA (paternal origin) is correlated
with Assur, the son of Shem. That would make me Semitic.
But of course people would probably call me anti-Semitic
for complaining about a rabbi. Anyway, according to my
Gedmatch results, I have significant admixture from the
Red Sea region. I also have a little sub-Saharan DNA, which
would make me partially Hamitic. My mitochondrial DNA
is found at the highest percentage among Ashkenazi Jews,
which means I could potentially be halachically Jewish. Oh,
Kanye West tweeted something yesterday about attacking
Jews or something. I wonder if he is going to pull a Roseanne
Barr or if he just doesn't care. Roseanne is Jewish. I like her.

Oh, speaking of black people, I hope I didn't trigger you with the
use of the n-word. I guess the world isn't ready for that kind of
post racist ideology. See, that's better, isn't it? Seriously, though,
if I were to ever procreate, it would be with a black woman.
Some of the mixed people I've talked to say they get shit from
both sides of the aisle, but at least they'd be more aware. And
I think mixed people are generally more aesthetically pleasing
than anyone else. But that's just me. It's the same with most

animals, I think. Are there any ugly animal hybrids? I just know I'm pretty interbred, and I need to add something fresh to the blood line. Just kidding, no one gives a fuck about my blood line except possibly obsessed fans of the serial killer who murdered several members of my family back in the 50s. But let's not test the waters.

Amy let me smoke some of her weed because I have a spot on my groin. It's a little white spot. I'm not sure if it's Herpes or an ingrown hair. I hope it's the latter. I already have one STD I don't know what to do with. Yes, I ended that sentence with a preposition. It was a difficult decision. Oh wait, I'm high. I'm supposed to be typing everything that's in my brain. That's almost impossible though. Niggers. See, people will stone me if I do that too much. I've already had kidney stones. Maybe that was God stoning me. It runs in the family.

My dad's dad might've been in the KKK. We don't really know. My dad said when he was a kid he thought my granddad had burnt a cross in the front yard of a neighbor's house because she had been sleeping around with other men. My ex-boyfriend's great-grandfather was on the run from the KKK. He had to change his name. They didn't like that he was running around with black folk. Interestingly, my ex's dad was a grand master, I think. I don't quote me on that. I do know that two men with different names are considered to be the grandparents of him and other people he matched with on AncestryDNA. And everyone has the same story that he lost his legs when he was hit by a train. It's an interesting mystery.

The first person I kissed was a black boy. It was kindergarten, and he just planted one on me. I wonder how he's doing. I looked him up on Facebook a while back. I also spoke with an old friend of his, and seemed to have been hinted that he might be gay. I don't know. My old best friend and roommate were black. She's the one I wanted to mate with. She doesn't think I'm racist. I feel like she would know—so would several other black friends of mine. But Yva said saying that I have black friends is a racist thing to say. Fuck Yva. Yva has no friends because she's a goddamn cunt.

No, really, I hope the best for her. Maybe editing Sweet 75's Wikipedia page will bring her publicity. In this day and age, I can imagine it would only make me look bad. Oh well. I'm not interested in the hive-mind, anyway. But it would be cool if Yva got famous again. It's about time. She's a fucking diva, anyway. She needs it. She has the ego of an upper class white lesbian. And by that I mean she needs to be underground famous with a small following and invitations to intimate gatherings where she'll be given lots of attention but not too much. I do care about Yva. She just really, really hurt my feelings, obviously. I think I'm going to get my friend Red to try to talk to her for me since he's a strong, intelligent black man who knows me fairly well. I mean, he knows my thoughts and opinions on pretty much everything, at least—especially this subject, I'm pretty sure. I've definitely had a lot of conversational hours with him. He's my dead boyfriend's sister's roommate. I should stop calling him my dead boyfriend, but he's not my ex-boyfriend because we never broke up. And he's not my boyfriend because he's not living. So I don't know what else to call him except Josh.

Anyway, I feel like exploring this "nigger" subject a little more. I should go hang out with them when I'm in town this week. I have to be at the college Wednesday to rehearse for some Veteran's Day affair. I feel like my dad is happy about that, since he's a veteran and all. In fact, if it weren't for the war, I wouldn't exist let alone be as fucked up as I am. Thanks, Ho Chi Minh.

I think I might be dying. Daniel and I agreed that could make my book better. He said it would definitely put a time frame on it. Maybe I should go to the doctor. Maybe it's just Herpes or an ingrown hair and not cancer. I don't know. I'm okay with dying of cancer, though. I just want them to give me some really good drugs. I want cancer, damnit. Daniel says his dad would tell him to go get a job if he had cancer. He sells timber or something in Alabama.

I'm hungry. I got a to-go plate from the gas station earlier, but I only ate a chicken leg and a few bites of macaroni and cheese and lima beans. I thought they were butter beans. I don't really understand the difference. Aw, Amy's on the phone with her sister. That's cool. They're talking about Amy's other daughter. We've been worried about her because there was a photo of her and her ex-boyfriend on instagram with her face blacked out, but she's okay. Okay, Daniel and I are going to go get some Benzedrex.

I just remembered my neighbors are black. I'm staying in a duplex. They've been here for years. I forgot they were black, to be honest. They're clearly black, though. I need to talk to them about whether or not it's okay for me to use the n-word in my book.

Fuck, I'm stoned. I got some really good weed and dabs from someone who I don't know if I can mention. I mean, I mentioned him in my last book, but I don't think I mentioned this aspect of him, and I don't know if he would mind, and I care about what he thinks, so I won't.

Blah blah blah. I got really high and made an awesome song and chatted with Cash for a while. Cash isn't his real name, but he said to call him that. That's what he's going to name his kid if he has another son. Anyway, he's like a straight brother who has let me watch him hook up with girls before without being ancestral, I guess.

I'm listening to my music. I like it, even though it makes me feel kind of isolated in the world. It's cold in my room. I have to leave the fan on so I can smoke, and the window is cracked open. And it's finally fall. I'm ready for that Benzedrex to wear off so I can sleep. I wonder if Daniel is still awake.

CHAPTER XXI

Fuck it. Well, I had gone a couple days without writing, and then I wrote a chapter. But apparently someone typed over 40,000 slashes, so I just cleared the whole file instead of dealing with it. Oh well. It's probably a good thing. I had said something I shouldn't have said. I had given my word to someone I wouldn't tell anyone about what happened, and I mentioned it, even though I didn't mention names or super important details. But still. People could've still figured it out.

Jett and I are going to see IC3PEAK in Underground Atlanta on Wednesday. They're this really awesome Russian band. They were supposed to be playing in Hell at the Masquerade, but the location got moved at the last minute for some reason. I asked Daniel if he thinks they're working for the government, and he doesn't think so. I was just wondering how they were able to get out of Russia. I guess they went to Turkey or something first. I think that's what Jett speculated. Who knows. It's just speculation. One of their videos is in support of the Ukrainian people, though. Just check out their music. Their videos are beautiful. And their lyrics are amazing. I love them.

Oh, an article came out today on CNN about the Princess of Orange. Apparently she had to move back into the palace due to security concerns. I hope I'm not one of those concerns. Her mother was quoted lamenting how her daughter couldn't experience student life like the other students. I sent another email suggesting she spend a semester anonymously here in Milledgeville. Daniel thinks I'm probably on a list now somewhere. I just hope it's a good list. Daniel is so pessimistic when it comes to my dreams.

Ha, Daniel and I were laughing about how instead of Princess and the Pea it might be Princess and the Benzedrex Container. Just kidding. We actually went to Walmart today, and I think they stopped carrying it. I'm just smoking weed right now. I do okay with that. I wonder if the princess's parents would be okay with that? I wonder if they would be okay with me. Are you supposed to capitalize "princess" every time? I don't know. I don't know shit about royal protocol. Can I say "shit"? I'm thinking about sending copies of my books to her when I'm done.

They probably just trashed my message as soon as they got it, just like everyone else who thinks they're above me somehow. Oh well. I'm just going to smoke more weed instead of meditating on slitting my wrists.

Okay, I smoked some more. I was thinking about how this book should be more meta, and then I thought about how I was just talking to Jett on the phone after having given my Jet girls (the girls at the Jet gas station) a copy of my book. Well, I gave one of the multi-colored-hair girls the book, but I signed it to both of them. She said she read a lot, though. I don't know any of their names, but I like them a lot. I have a feeling I'm probably more astrologically compatible with the one to whom I actually physically gave the book, though. That would be interesting to see. I'll see if I can remember to ask about their birthdays the next time I go back there.

I just don't know. I don't know about anything. Now I'm concerned about this Princess of Orange thing. I hope they don't think I'm part of some criminal gang or something. It's just a coincidence that I wrote the song right before this happened, I hope. Linda Perry is playing on YouTube. 4 Non Blondes - "What's Up". Clementine used to date her. My mom gave me a bag of clementines last night along with some boiled peanuts and kiwi fruit. I ate all the good boiled peanuts and three of the clementines. They're tasty. The real one is too bitter. Ha. I sound like a lesbian. Now I want to hear that song Linda wrote for

Courtney Love.

I'm preheating the stove to make some steaks for Amy. She's been asking for them for days, but I haven't been in the best mood or here, really. But I'm finally doing it, so there's that. Amy's daughter and Clementine kissed once, I think. Clementine had a thing for her. I used to have a thing for guys Naomi had a thing for, which pissed Naomi a lot—especially when I would get drunk and fool around with them, which only happened like three times maybe. Once was an accident, I think. Long story.

Anyway, Kurt is singing now. "Man Who Sold the World". I wonder if anyone has noticed my change on Sweet 75's Wikipedia yet. It's still there. Maybe I should take it down. Oh well. It's an interesting experiment, at least, and it's all true, as far as I know. Damn, these steaks are looking good. They're thick ribeyes, and I seared them on top of the stove before putting them in the oven and basting them with butter and garlic. Yum. Three more minutes. I wonder what Turkey and Nothing are doing tonight. I haven't seen them in days. I think and hope they've stopped doing meth. But on the other hand, some hard drugs would be kind of nice. I'd rather have opiates, though. Bad me. I'll just stick to my steak and weed. How about a glass of wine, at least? Too bad Daniel's an alcoholic.

I think I'm just being delusional. The steak was good, though. Anyway, I don't even think anyone in the Netherlands ever heard my song. Someone in England did, though. I think we're going to go get some Kratom. Supposedly Daniel's getting some money from his cryptocurrency exchange. We'll see. I wish the methadone clinic took my insurance. They were working on accepting it, but I never heard back from them. I should call them tomorrow. That would be ideal.

I just got off the phone with my old friend who works in Admissions at Mercer University. She says the princess should be an exchange student there. I think that's a great idea. By the way, this is the same friend who was the first person to identify my borderline personality disorder. Well, she was the first person who ever mentioned me having an "FP" (favorite person). She is very observant. Smart cookie. Mercer needs to keep her. Speaking of which, maybe I should just start telling people I'm borderline instead of schizo. Borderline probably sounds better, even though in reality it's probably way worse. It seems that way, at least, for me and everyone who knows me (except for others who have or understand the disorder).

Ugh, I have an ingrown hair (I hope) in my crotchal area. I was sitting here moaning uncomfortably while fondling it, and Daniel said I was acting like the dudes in prison. Now we're listening to "Bad Romance" by Lady Gaga because that's how we roll. Goddamn, I know the Princess is going to be smitten when she reads this.

Okay, so, a couple hours have passed since I last wrote. Daniel and I went to get cigarettes at the Jet, and I decided we should go downtown and try to get free drinks. We did. The bartender made a mistake on a cocktail, so it was mine. And Daniel got a beer. We met some pretty neat people and had some interesting conversations. I learned a lot about TikTok from this nifty chick, and her man or whatever tried to get me to adopt a kitten. Amy won't have it, though, even though I told her Lil Bit told me she wanted a child. It's all black, just like her. Oh, and before we left, I hollered out the window and asked some random girl walking down the sidewalk for a song suggestion, and it was "Hallucinogens". That's a pretty damn good song.

I'm getting high, of course. We finally decided to grind it to be more efficient. We've probably wasted hundreds of dollars not grinding it. Oh well. I really want to know if the Princess has listened to my song. I should probably remember what her actual name is. I think it's Amelia. That sounds right. I'm probably wrong. Oh well. Maybe we can still be friends.

I was thinking about subtitling this book "Marry Me, Princess of Orange". Is that too much? I think I said I was going to subtitle my last book "Not for the Wholesome", and I never did. Oh well. That's a lot of "Oh wells", huh? I'm unsure about grammar sometimes. Oh well. Damnit. Stop it. I can't. I'm sorry. Don't be sorry. It's okay. Shh. It'll all be over soon. Don't say that. That's creepy. Oh wait, that's how I'm supposed to write this book—stream-of-consciousness. Train-of-thought, which I rarely have been doing for some reason in this sequel. That's pretty disappointing. Bad me. I should kill myself. Just kidding. That's just what my brain said. Oh yeah, I need weed for this. That's what I need. I need to be stoned all the time. Otherwise I think too much about what I'm thinking about and forget to write what I'm thinking. Does that make sense? If I think about it too much, I'll forget what I was supposed to say, so I won't think. I'll just type. Just type. I wonder how long this paragraph is now. Grinding this weed was definitely the way to go. Should I correct my typos? I just backspaced to change "the" to "'the". Actually, I just backspaced several times to fix several typos as I was trying to explain to you what I did when I had to backspace, so maybe some backspaces are necessary. Otherwise it would be an absolutely aesthetic nightmare. I noticed in my last book there were a couple typos that weren't very pretty. Speaking of aesthetics, I should probably start a new paragraph now.

That's better. How many words do I have in this chapter now? Let me check. 1693. I wonder how many words that last paragraph had in relation to my average paragraph. That was nice. I should do it more often. I wonder if people like that style of rambling? Hmm. Who could I ask? Daniel hasn't even read my book yet. He read the first paragraph and said that it had a hook. It wasn't intended. I wonder if any of my music has hooks. I don't try to put them in there, although I've had people tell me I should put hooks in my songs. I told you about the guy at Short Mountain who told me that, right? Shit, I don't remember what I've told you and what I haven't. That's a problem.

Should I go search through my last book and see what I've mentioned already? I wish I could just ask you or myself or whatever. Yeah, the guy with green eyes and long hair at Short Mountain. He shed a tear when he heard my music and said he hadn't heard real music in so long. But his voice seemed to change when he sternly told me I had to put hooks in my songs if I wanted to make any money.

I was going to go to Short Mountain for Fall Gathering, but I didn't make it. I was supposed to do something else, too, but I forgot what. Oh well. Oh well. Oh well. I don't want to be like Captain Hook, damnit. I want to be Peter Pan. Or Tinkerbell. Or their offspring, really. I don't know who the fuck I am, to be honest. I'm Jupiter Davidson. Jove for short. That's who I am, damnit. That's who I am.

My name is Jove. I was born just after sunset at the end of Yom HaShoah, although Hitler and I share the same birthday on the Christian Calendar. Or the Julian calendar. Same thing, I guess. I wonder if I'll ever be able to convert one day. Maybe I can just prove that I'm already a Jew with my mitochondrial DNA.

I could also prove my connection with my higher self (the planet) by correlating electromagnetic radiation with the results from an MRI or something. I'm not an astrophysicist or a neuroscientist, so I'm not exactly sure how that would work, but I know it would. We're all connected to cosmological bodies. We are cosmological bodies. Just some of our connections are different than others'.

I have a cough. I hope I don't have Covid. I also don't want lung cancer, even though I know I already said I wanted cancer. I'd rather not have that kind of cancer. I want to be able to breathe, at least. Fuck. Life sucks. Death sucks. Life is dying. Dying is life. It's one and the same, although Rabbi Friedman says the soul can't die because living things can only live. I just wrote a song along a similar vein, pun fitting but not intended (if you listen to it, you'll understand, maybe). It's called "Mercurochrome". I like it. I hope you like it. I hope if you like it we can be friends. If you don't like it, I hope you at least enjoy this book.

Wow, that was kind of rude. I guess we can still be friends even if you don't enjoy my song. Jett used to hate my ukulele and my Broadway voice, although she likes my music now. I don't really use those much anymore, though. Speaking of which, I kind of want to listen to my own music a little. Amy's ex-husband came in earlier as I was listening to it, and he just looked at the TV with this horribly disgusted face. It kind of hurt my soul a little. Oh well, I don't think he liked me to begin with. He was also drunk. He did diagnose my car problem, though, which was really nice of him.

Yeah, I need a lot of work done on my car, though, in addition to a new tire. I actually got a new tire and found out I need new struts and a new engine coil. I ordered the engine coil and paid off my title pawn, and now I have about $3 in SpotMe left on Chime. I have an Apple Magic Keyboard I could sell, though. And I have an antique copy of the Declaration of Independence that's only really worth about $400. This guy at an antique shop offered me $50 for it. I wonder how much the pawn shop guys would offer me. I wish I were in Vegas. I'd go to Pawn Stars. Daniel thinks that I should call Pawn Stars. Maybe I will. Maybe we'll just go to Las Vegas and try to sell it. Oh fuck, he can't fly because he doesn't have an ID. Maybe I'll just do it. My lovely high school friend lives there. She's a real estate agent and is absolutely stunning. I am so happy her life is good. She deserves it. She was always good to me. And she finally got her tits. You'd never even know. (I guess. I don't really notice boobies unless they're extreme or something.) Anyway, yeah, grinding the weed is definitely the way to go. For sure.

Daniel has been talking to all these Russian-looking women. Oh, they moved the location of IC3PEAK to some really sketchy warehouse looking place. Amy thinks I need to ask for a refund, but I don't know. I'm a little weirded out. I just don't want to be tortured, really. Anyway, there's this one girl who he's been talking to who claims to be a porn star, and he says we're going to have a double wedding. I wonder if the Princess will go for that.

I should Google her name. Maybe it's Catherina? How about AC? I'm just going to call her that. I like AC. I wonder if they have AC in the Netherlands. Does it get hot there? I have no idea what the climate is like. I'd imagine it's somewhere between temperate and subarctic. I forgot what kind of climate I live in, but I found out recently it's not actually temperate.

Anyway, now we're at Turkey and Nothing's house. Nothing had heartburn from spaghetti, so I had to bring her some Prilosec. Amy gave me two. I'm sitting in the corner typing while they converse about some sort of drug, I think. Yeah. I don't know what kind. It sounds hallucinogenic. I still don't know, and they've been talking for a while. Now they're talking about someone doing it in a chicken plant in Dothan, Alabama. Someone smashed ten cars on it, apparently. I'm going to tell them this conversation is going in my book. Or should I? I should probably find out what drug they're talking about. Okay, it's spice. That makes sense.

Ugh, I smoked a little meth, and it made me really horny, so I spent the past couple hours or so looking at naked guys on Reddit. I took a shower and masturbated. We're still at Turkey and Nothing's. They're taking a break from discussing cryptocurrency. Withdrawals just opened on Daniel's exchange. He's trying to put in a sell order. We'll see what happens. The liquidity is pretty low right now, so who knows what will happen. Maybe nothing. Maybe a few nights at the Four Seasons. Time will tell. I miss the Four Seasons. I haven't been there in years.

Actually it's been a while since I've experienced anything above a middle class lifestyle except when my mom and I went to Los Angeles earlier this year and went to a deliciously expensive Italian restaurant in West Hollywood. I guess I should tell you what happened, even though my mom doesn't want me to write about the family. I guess I already did in my last book. I don't know what I should do. It's a tough decision. Right now my relationship with my mother is okay, so I'll just say that we had a disagreement which got blown out of proportion, but we're okay now. We're okay. I love my mother, but when we clash, we clash heavily.

I'm trying to get Nothing to sing a duet with me. I think her voice would mesh well with mine. It is interesting. I heard a voice similar to it on Jupiter Davidson Radio or whatever on Apple Music. I'm so happy their algorithm finally paired my music with other music like mine, whatever that may be called. Or maybe it was a human being? Who knows. Either way, they did a fantastic job. They should have the Apple Music engineers train the Siri engineers or something—no offense, Siri engineers. I'm sure it has something to do with the fact that I'm comparing Siri to Hey Google, and Google's informational database is vastly superior to Apple's. I wonder how much access Apple has to Google's. Maybe that's the impediment.

Nothing is mad that I made her name Nothing. Okay, she said she's just picking. That's cool. I like the name. It was the name of my favorite character in Lost Souls by Poppy Z. Brite. That's one of the few books I've ever read more than once and enjoyed. I highly recommend it if you like alternative, queer vampires. Poppy is amazing. I guess he's still going by Poppy. Maybe he's not. I'm not really sure. I'm actually not even entirely sure if he's still going by he. I should've said "they". Oh well. Oh well. Oh well. I've said worse, clearly.

We were just talking about peyote. Did I mention in my last book the time I took 2c-p in NYC and ended up covered in paint in Manhattan in the middle of the night handing out tangerines to sex workers? That was a very fun and intense night. I wonder what happened to that guy I had sex with whose face morphed. He was an artist. I forgot his name. I think he was famous— well, however famous you have to be to get an apartment in Brooklyn paid for you because of your art. He'll probably be more famous after he's dead. I've never actually seen any of his art other than the "painting" he made on the canvas on the floor when we were tripping, even though a lot of it ended up on me.

And then there was Piss. I remember his name. He was so cute. He had a tear tattoo below his eye. I got to watch his legs as he was getting a blowjob from his girlfriend in the subway station. I wish I could've seen more. I wonder what tribe he belongs to. So beautiful. I hope someone who knows him reads this.

It's 10:30 at night the next day, and I still haven't slept other than about a five minute cat nap. I might try to do that soon.

CHAPTER XXII

I still haven't fucking slept. It's been days. I just took a bunch of Kratom. We're out of weed. I'm in a terrible mood with pretty bad suicidal ideation. I messaged my stuck up bitch of an ex-girlfriend with a screenshot of where I mentioned her in my last book, and she wasn't thrilled. She said she would've rather not known. I guess some people never change. I really hope Russia nukes the fuck out of us. I'm ready for the end. The world can go fuck itself.

I have no good reason to live. Everything is shittie and painful and boring. People are shit. I am shit. I am people. I wish I weren't such a pussy, otherwise I'd do it myself. It'd be easier if I had a gun, but they're expensive, and Daniel claims they won't give me one since I've been in a state mental hospital before. I don't know if that's true.

I'm thinking about driving to California when I get paid. That's two weeks away, though. I guess I could go ahead and sell my MacBook and stuff for gas money. I'm thinking about getting rid of the Internet, too. I hate the Internet. I wish it had never existed. I wish computers had never existed. They've really fucked everything up, even though it might be necessary for God's final plan, if there is a god and a final plan, at least. I guess I'm on the fence at this point. I need some hard drugs. Some heroin would be fucking amazing. I haven't had any in so long. I have fond memories of shooting up with Piss in a Bed Stay laundromat bathroom in the middle of the night and then skipping through Brooklyn. Good times, good times. I'm surprised I didn't get Hepatitis from him. He told me he had it, but I was being self-destructive and used his needle anyway.

My arm swelled up in these patches like quilted toilet paper for some reason. But it still felt great. Heroin also reminds me of my old friend Derek. I used to let him shoot me up because it was kind of erotic for me. He was so cute. He tried to get me to have a threesome with him and his baby's mama but she ended up going into labor that night. That would've been weird.

I'm so ready to go see IC3PEAK. Three more days. They're so damn good. I just read where they were banned in Russia from having concerts. Fuck Putin.

I'm thinking about adding this to my old book and re-publishing it with a different cover. I really need to make some money. I wonder if I have a chance. I totally want to sell out. I need new teeth, something bad. My front tooth is about to go. That's going to suck. I barely smile as it is. I have shittie fucking genetics. Thanks, inbreeding ancestors.

Amy's going to Atlanta tomorrow, and I'm broke, which means I'll probably run out of cigarettes at some point, and she won't be here for me to use her vape. What am I going to do? I know I need to quit smoking, but I was going to wait until my life wasn't so shittie. What if that doesn't happen until I quit smoking, though? Goddamn catch-22s.

I'm so exhausted, but I still can't sleep. I've been uploading what I've written this-go-round to my original document. I think I'm just going to publish a second edition with this "epilogue". I know, eight chapters, at least, is a little much for an epilogue, but whatever. It is what it is. Thanks, Traci.

The first girl to ever read my book said she wanted more, so I'm giving you more. I just feel bad for everyone who bought the first sixteen or whatever chapters of my book. Maybe one day the incomplete first edition will be worth some money. It'll most likely be after I'm dead. That's how it goes.

I have over 77k words now. That's a fairly decent-sized book. Where am I going with it, though? Someone on some self-publishing Discord server said I should resolve it somehow, I think. I guess that's what they were saying. But how am I going to resolve my clusterfuck of a life? I could go to California. I could kill myself. I could abandon the Internet. I could do all of the above, at least metaphorically. I don't know who should die, though—Jupiter or... who am I? I don't know who I am.

Nancy Sinatra's "Bang Bang" is playing now. I was telling Daniel earlier how I wanted to be like Uma Thurman in Kill Bill and chop off assholes' heads for a living. I need a katana or something. Is that terrible? My sword would be terribly swift. Yes, I'm quoting "Battle Hymn of the Republic". Did you know that was originally a Yankee fight song?

We're out of weed. I'm smoking what's left of a Delta 8 pen. And now he's gone. I don't know why. And till this day, sometimes I cry. He didn't even say goodbye. He didn't take the time to lie. Bang, bang. He shot me down. Bang, bang, I hit the ground. That awful sound. Bang, bang. My baby shot me down.

Baby. That's what Lori #2's daughter called my ex-boyfriend when she was little because I called him that all the time. I was so madly in love with him. I would've taken him back even after he broke my ribs, had he not threatened to destroy me if I ever messaged him again. I shouldn't have abandoned him in Los Angeles, but I was in severe pain. Getting your ass kicked is no joke. He was a zombie on The Walking Dead. He ended up getting arrested for battery. I guess he did it to someone else. Did I mention him in my last "book"? I guess it's the same book now. This is the evolution of the meta-memoir.

Cowboy Junkies is playing now. Sweet Jane. Now I really want some heroin again. That would be nice. Any opiate would suffice, really. It's cold in here. I need to find my jacket or a blanket. I'm on my bed. There's a blanket behind me. I'm high, I guess. Fuck.

So how are we going to end this? There needs to be a resolution. What kind of resolution? I have no idea what to do. Someone just tapped me on Grindr. They want a cuddle buddy. That would be nice. I wonder if they're attractive. Oh, it's a very large black man. I hooked up with this really hot black guy recently, but that's all I can say. I gave him my word I wouldn't tell anyone. I'm not really into black bears, though, I don't think. I'm not into bears in general, really, although I do enjoy their company. I did cuddle with one at Short Mountain once. He was a cub, though. It was okay until he fell asleep on top of me. I almost suffocated. Maybe I should sleep on this—this decision, I mean, about how this should end. Or maybe I should just go ahead and end it. Yeah, that sounds nice. I'm just tired.

I think I'm going off the Internet-grid and drive out to Los Angeles and live in my car. If it doesn't work out, I'll drown myself in the ocean. That's what I was going to do a few weeks ago before I committed myself. I don't think it would be a terrible way to go. It's like going back into the womb, only saltier. I'm just so tired. I'm tired of life. I'm tired of the world. I'm tired of myself. I'm tired of hurting in every possible way and somehow still feeling empty. The pain just pushes me further into the ground. "Wicked Game" is playing now. My ex—the one that broke my ribs—used to get me to sing this to him while he fell asleep in the hammock in the back yard in Compton. That was a nice time. I didn't feel empty then. And there were loquat trees. I miss those loquats. That's what I'm going to do. I'm going to go pick some loquats in California. Come find me on the boardwalk. If you've read this all, I love you.

I miss my Grandma. I miss Randall. I miss Josh. I miss Sharon. I miss so many dead people. If I knew I could join them, I would in a heartbeat. But I don't know. I have no idea, really. And that's what sucks. Hopefully my car will make it to LA. Am I doing the right thing? Who do I ask? I wish there were a god who would talk to me. What if I'm really a god? What if I'm really Jupiter? What if everything really is connected? It's all so fucked up and dramatic, really. It's exhausting. I don't even care anymore. Maybe I was going to repeat the same mistake by mating with a human princess. Or was it a mistake? Who the fuck knows? The world of my mind is definitely not for the wholesome. It might even be a little much for the corrupt. C'est la goddamn vie.

They say Moses wrote about his own death in the Torah. While that's probably bullshit, maybe it's not. I'd like to write about my death. But I'm no prophet, as far as I know. Speaking of Moses, I talked to mine earlier. I told him I was going to California. He understood. He had bad teeth, too.

So that's what I'm going to do. I've made my resolution. I'm publishing this, I'm driving to Los Angeles, and if I don't find some sort of solace or happiness there, I'm walking into the ocean. Fuck, no, that's bullshit. I'm too much of a pussy to do that. Fuck. I don't know what I'm going to do. I don't know how to resolve this. That's too much goddamn pressure. I can't deal. Fuck. Goddamnit. I hate people. I hate expectations. Fuck off with that shit. Just let me do what the fuck I want with my own goddamn art. If you don't like it, go eat a donkey dick. I said it. Still, if you've read this far, I love you—whatever that word may mean. I love that you have been interested enough in my mind to read this far. Maybe we can be friends.

Fuck. I feel like shit. If I had a gun right now, there's a huge chance I would pull the trigger. I'm tired of hurting, and life is probably only going to get worse. I just want to be a baby again. I miss my mommy. Fuck, shedding a few tears helped bring some slight relief, at least. Someone put me out of my misery, please. Just do it humanely, okay? That's all I ask. I need a damn cigarette.

Fuck. I really need a drink. That would be nice. Some sleep would be good, too. I fucking hate meth. Maybe I should go to rehab. I don't know. I need a drink. That would be perfect. Maybe I should just become an alcoholic. Damn, now I have to pee. I sharted in my pajamas earlier. It's been a common occurrence ever since I had my gallbladder removed. The opiate withdrawal doesn't help, either. That's what I need—more Kratom. It's just so fucking bitter and gross. I always have to swallow my puke when I take it.

I just got the resonance feeling that "Everybody Knows" by Leonard Cohen is about me. Fuck. I knew it. Shit. What am I supposed to do about that? This is such a shittie part to play. I wouldn't recommend it. At least there are tears. The tears help the pain. From the bloody cross on top of Calvary to the beach at Malibu. Everybody knows. What a cosmic joke. The film is a saddening bore because I wrote it ten times before. Bowie knew. I met his alleged adopted son at Union Square in Manhattan once. Who the fuck cares?

What am I supposed to do this go round? Or does it even matter? What will be will be, I guess. There's no stopping our old friend Time. I don't think he's too happy with me. Who made this? What is this? What are we in? It's ridiculous, really. It's a mess. Maybe I should start blessing more and cursing less. Maybe I should do a lot of things, but I don't. If you could only be in my head right now. Too much. Too much. Too much. I'm done. I'm just done. Is this the end? Is this the end? I'm such a shittie messiah. Bless it.

Made in the USA
Middletown, DE
28 October 2022

13429212R00128